When Kiwis Fly:

A Sports Tour of Great Britain

By Duncan Perkinson

When Kiwis Fly:
A Sports Tour of Great Britain

By Duncan Perkinson

First published in Great Britain in 2012 by The Derby Books Publishing Company Limited,
3 The Parker Centre, Derby, DE21 4SZ.

This paperback edition published in Great Britain in 2013 by DB Publishing,
an imprint of JMD Media Ltd

ISBN 978-1-78091-058-1

Printed and bound in the UK by Copytech (UK) Ltd Peterborough

Contents

Acknowledgements

There are many people I'd like to acknowledge as they have been very helpful as I've written this book.

Without your assistance, encouragement, belief, words of wisdom, patience and inspiration, this project would not have got off the ground and I wouldn't have smiled as much while I worked.

Mike Berry, Richard Barton and Campbell Ogilvie – thanks for the road trips to many of these venues.

To Martin Heyes – thank you for instilling belief.

Rich, Nige and Frank – thanks for the 'brainstorming' sessions over a pint.

Mike Thorpe and Stephen Hegh – a debt of gratitude to you both.

I'd like to thank everyone at DB Publishing. I'd also like to say thanks to Paul Dalling and Alison Dutton.

A great big thank you to everyone at the venues within the book who provided me with guidance, advice, information and even occasionally tickets! There are so many but special thanks to Kirsty Ball, Emma Owen, Clive Everton, Kurt Pittman, Peter Greville, Ellen Morgan and Graham Emmerson.

To my Mum and Dad for allowing me to stay up late and watch sport when it was past my bedtime. It turns out I wasn't just watching TV, I was undertaking research.

To my late granddad and to my Uncle John who took me to so many sporting events growing up in New Zealand.

To Doreen, thank you for your flexibility and for all your help right from the start of this project.

To John and Sofie. I love you both. Thank you kiddos.

And to my darling Jeanette… Without you this book would be a short article, my smile would be smaller and my life less joyful. The adventures and the laughing will always continue. I love you.

Finally, I'd like to thank you as a reader for picking this book up. My mission was to guide New Zealand travellers across the sports fields of Great Britain. This book is the map and I hope you learn, gasp, laugh and feel pride for New Zealand.

Dedication

My darling, You said yes and forever started

Introduction

Stadia across the UK are temples for sports fans. Places where crowds gather to worship at the feet of the gods on the pitch, track or course.

Sporting stadia are intrinsically linked to the culture, fabric and history of the UK. They have been playing golf at St Andrews for over 500 years – 300 years before New Zealand made it onto the map!

When Kiwis Fly tells the stories of dreams, hopes, disappointment and redemption. It is the story of New Zealand growing up as a nation in the sporting venues of Britain.

Sporting venues across Great Britain are wonderful. From the whispering to the ear splitting, the rickety to the state-of-the-art, they all have their own eccentricities, charms and quirks.

Great Britain has played a leading role in the formation of many sports and to visit these venues where the sport was 'born' is very special.

But, it is also wonderful to visit these venues because of the importance they have played in the sociological history of New Zealand.

New Zealand has closer historical links to Great Britain than anywhere else in the world. As a nation, New Zealand has matured on the sports fields of the 'motherland'. The founding forefathers left Great Britain on boats to form a nation. They had sports equipment with them and this became the glue, which started to meld New Zealand. It is because of British origins that Kiwis play rugby, golf, netball, hockey and cricket, not Boules, Handball and Sumo wrestling.

New Zealanders on tour have generally always acted with humility, dignity and pride. When combined with ferocity and competitiveness on the pitch, New Zealand has endeared itself to the British people. Across the UK people speak so warmly about New Zealand. They will reminisce about their trip or explain how they would love to go there one day.

This book endeavours to be a guide to where New Zealanders have succeeded. This book aims to accentuate the positives so venues where Kiwis have acted in an unbecoming style have been excluded. The stories from the pubs, bars, and hotel rooms can stay in the tabloid newspapers.

Venues have been split into regional sections. Wales, London and Scotland all have their own sections. The South West of England includes Gloucestershire, Wiltshire, Dorset, Somerset, Devon and Cornwall.

Yorkshire and the North East includes Yorkshire, West Yorkshire, Durham, but also Lincolnshire. The section titled the Midlands includes the counties from Northamptonshire up to Nottinghamshire, Derbyshire and Staffordshire.

The North West includes Lancashire, Cheshire and Cumbria as well as the Isle of Man, which while strictly not part of Great Britain is geographically closest to this area.

The South East section includes Oxfordshire, Buckinghamshire, Bedfordshire, Hertfordshire, Cambridgeshire, Norfolk, Suffolk, Essex, Kent, Surrey, East and West Sussex, Hampshire, the Isle of Wight and Berkshire.

The book includes many football and rugby grounds – and this demonstrates the importance of the two sports to the two countries. But there are many grounds where the All Blacks have played and many major British football grounds, which are not on the list.

Commonwealth and Empire Games venues where New Zealanders have claimed gold medals are all included as are the venues where New Zealanders have succeeded in major sporting Championships.

Annual British events where New Zealanders have previously succeeded have been included. Some of the venues in the book no longer exist but it has been important to include these in recognition of our sporting history.

There are no venues from Northern Ireland within the book – such as Ravenhill and The Ulster 200 – as this is a guidebook to Great Britain, not to the United Kingdom.

This book is about sporting venues so there are no hints as to the best places to watch sport and there are no suggestions as to the best places to play sport in Great Britain.

Every fan recognises the value of sporting debates and many readers will have excellent reasons for why certain venues should or should not be in the book.

The mission of this book when I started was to guide New Zealand travellers through the sports fields of Great Britain. This book is the map and with it I sincerely hope you will learn, gasp and laugh but most of all feel pride in your New Zealand heritage.

London

If you cannot find what you are looking for in London, check what it is you are looking for. One of the truly great cities in the world, London has it all.

It is home to some of the most iconic global sporting venues – Lord's, Wimbledon and Twickenham among others.

London is the first city to have ever hosted three Olympic Games. The 2012 version marked the city as a global centre of sport.

It is home to some of the great theatres and cinemas in and around Leicester Square.

The financial square mile of the City of London sees billions of pounds change hands every day – it is one of the major financial centres of the world.

The sights of the city are known across the world – The Tower of London, black cabs, Big Ben and red buses.

Culturally the city has great art galleries, theatres, clubs, concerts and museums.

The two Tate Galleries and the National Gallery are among the very best in the world. The British Museum is a treasure trove of the fascinating and thought provoking. The V & A Museum, the Natural History Museum, the

Science Museum and the Design Museum – you will be amazed at how much you can discover.

The city is home to British politics and from the public galleries it is possible to view the shouting matches in the House of Commons and the House of Lords.

Westminster Abbey is truly spectacular and some of the greatest people are buried there. Lord Ernest Rutherford is buried there, near to Sir Isaac Newton and Charles Darwin. The royal family have used the church for weddings from King Henry I in 1100 to Prince William in 2011.

Over the past years the leading London restaurants have forged a new reputation for British cuisine. There are over 50 Michelin starred restaurants across the city run by superstar chefs who have become celebrities themselves.

According to Benjamin Disraeli – the former Prime Minister: 'London is a roost for every bird,' so wherever you go in London, there is always something amazing to see, hear, taste or learn.

Alexandra Palace

Alexandra Palace Way, London, N22 7AY
www.alexandrapalace.com

This hill top Palace was built in the 1870s for the great British public to enjoy recreation and entertainment.

It needed to be built twice as a fire destroyed the building just 16 days after it was first built in 1873. It was then rebuilt and reopened in 1875.

Over the years, 'Ally Pally', as it is affectionately known, has hosted a wide range of events. You could have seen concerts, plays, Jazz Festivals, Antiques fairs, the Miss World Pageant, Ice Hockey and art exhibitions. Some of the singers and bands to have played at the Palace have included Gracie Fields, Pink Floyd, The Grateful Dead, Blur and more recently Jay-Z.

Historically, in the grounds of the Palace, there was a horse racing track until 1970 and cricket and football were played in the park. The Masters Snooker Tournament moved to Alexandra Palace in 2012.

But for many sports fans, Ally Pally, is now the home of the PDC Darts championship.

As the war between the two rival darts organisations BDO and PDC intensified, the PDC struck a blow when they announced they would be moving their World Championship event from the Circus Tavern to Alexandra Palace because it could hold a much bigger audience.

As the event is held over the two weeks of Christmas and New Year, at the height of the British cold season, fans ironically sing along to Chase the Sun. More than 2,500 fans chant, drink, sing, drink, dress up, drink, bring along funny signs and drink.

Since moving to Alexandra Palace in 2008, New Zealanders Warren Parry, Alan Bolton, Warren French, Phillip Hazel and Preston Ridd have all competed but none have made it past the first round.

Boleyn Ground, London

Green Street, London, E13 9AZ
www.whufc.com

This is the home ground to London's East End football club, West Ham United. The stadium is more commonly referred to as Upton Park.

The Boleyn name has a ghostly past – as some people believe the area is haunted by one of Anne Boleyn's maids who died in childbirth. There is no doubt that the stadium was named because it is on the site of Boleyn's former home – Green Street House.

The Hammers, as they are known, were formed as a professional side in 1900 and joined the Football League just after World War One. They have never won the League title, but have won the FA Cup three times – most recently in 1980. That was a day for *Blowing Bubbles* – the song Hammers fans always sing and one that has a history that dates back to the 1920s.

West Ham's most well known ex-player is Bobby Moore who was a product of the Academy of Football and played 544 games for the club over 16 years. Moore was captain of the England team that won the World Cup in 1966 and a stand at the ground is named in his honour.

New Zealand's Winston Reid signed for West Ham after the 2010 World Cup.

Moore is one of a long list of graduates from the West Ham Academy who have gone on to greatness. As well as Moore, the two goal scorers in the World Cup final, Martin Peters and Geoff Hurst, were also graduates. More recently, Rio Ferdinand, Frank Lampard, Joe Cole, Glen Johnson, Michael Carrick and Jermain Defoe have all come out of the Academy and gone on to play for the England national side.

In 2010 after the World Cup in South Africa, New Zealand's Winston Reid signed for West Ham. After making 12 appearances and scoring in an FA Cup win over Burnley in his first season, the centre-back helped the Hammers to gain promotion to the Premier League in 2011/12, starting the Championship Play-off final victory over Blackpool at Wembley Stadium.

West Ham have ambitions to leave the Boleyn Ground and may move to the new Olympic stadium but as with many new stadia, there are many bureaucratic hurdles to climb before this becomes a reality.

Christ's College

East End Road, Finchley, London, N2 0SE
www.ccfplus.com

Kiwis have a lot to thank this north London College for, as it was here that the father of rugby in New Zealand learnt the game that would play such a major part in the country's development.

Charles Monro was the son of the then speaker of the New Zealand Parliament, Sir David Monro and went to England to study at the College between 1867 and 1869. Upon his return to New Zealand, he organised the first ever game of rugby on New Zealand soil between his old school, Nelson College and Nelson Football Club.

Monro was not a great player – he had played in Christ's College's second XV – but it was his organisation that became the launching point for New Zealand's national game.

The game was played at the Botanics Park on 14 May 1870, there were 18 players on each team, a crowd of around 200 watched, the town team won 2-0 and rugby in New Zealand was up and running.

Monro is now honoured with a statue that stands at the Rugby Museum in Palmerston North and the annual NZRFU award to the volunteer of the year is named in his honour.

A re-enactment of that first game was staged in Nelson just prior to the start of the 2011 World Cup with players dressed in period costume, while high teas and cucumber sandwiches were served.

Rugby in South Africa also has claims to the Christ's College in London as it was there that R.W. Shepstone Giddy went to school and he has claims to be the founder of rugby in South Africa.

The school's links to rugby are strong as William Carpmael was at the school between 1876 and 1883 and he was the founder and first president of the Barbarian Football Club – traditionally the last game of a New Zealand tour to the UK.

Craven Cottage

Craven Cottage, Stevenage Road, London, SW6 6HH
www.fulhamfc.com

For many New Zealand fans, this is often the first taste of top-flight football they will see. As many New Zealanders live in west London, Fulham, QPR and Brentford are the most convenient teams to support.

Craven Cottage has been Fulham's home since 1896 and the stadium is on the banks of the river Thames. In one of the prettiest locations, with a picturesque stadium, it is a joy to watch football at Craven Cottage.

The ground has a capacity of fewer than 27,000 so is one of the smallest grounds in the top flight. The stadium is named after an old cottage that was previously on the wooded site.

On the field, Fulham's best years were through the 1960s when the team played in the top flight and was led by Johnny Haynes – nicknamed 'The Maestro' by the fans. He played 657 games for the club after signing as a schoolboy in 1950. After his death in 2005 a stand at Craven Cottage was named in his honour. The Johnny Haynes Stand was built in 1905, is the oldest stand in the Football League and is a listed building.

The club was relegated in 1968 and did not return to the top flight until 2001. The club's fightback had started under the ownership of Mohamed Al Fayed who bought the club in 1997 – just before his son Dodi tragically died in a car crash with Diana, Princess of Wales.

Fulham have solidified their position as a top-flight side over the decade and went to the final of the Europa League in 2010 – losing to Atletico Madrid in extra-time.

New Zealand's Simon Elliott played 13 games for Fulham during the 2005-06 season under then manager Chris Coleman but he suffered an injury, missed the following season and was then released by the club.

The ground was used for football preliminaries for the 1948 London Olympics. Australia has regularly used Craven Cottage for international matches as many Socceroos are based in Europe. New Zealand lost 1-0 to Australia in June 2005 at Craven Cottage.

Fulham Rugby League Club was the predecessor to Harlequins Rugby

League side and played at Craven Cottage when they were formed in 1980. They spent four years at the ground, before moving to Crystal Palace, Chiswick Polytechnic and then in 2006 to Twickenham Stoop. Over time the club changed its names to London Crusaders, London Broncos then Harlequins and then back to London Broncos.

Crystal Palace

Venue no longer exists:
Approximate Address: Ledrington Road, London, SE19 2BB

This was formerly the greatest sporting venue in the capital. It was superseded by Wembley Stadium but prior to this, the great and the good watched the best play at the Palace.

The name Crystal Palace comes from the cast iron and glass building that had been built for the Great Exhibition of 1851 and was originally situated in Hyde Park.

It was then moved to an affluent south London suburb called Sydenham Hill in 1854. Over time, the area became known as Crystal Palace.

In 1911, the Crystal Palace hosted The Festival of the Empire. This festival was to celebrate the coronation of King George V and commemorated all things great about the Empire. Four New Zealand athletes competed as part of the festivities – Malcolm Champion, Guy Haskins, Ron Opie and William Woodger.

At the 1911 Festival of Empire, Riki Papakura was performing as a Maori Warrior. While in the UK, he was recommended to Warrington Rugby League Club by Frank Shugars and former New Zealand representative Massa Johnston.

Papakura played centre for Warrington's first grade team on 14 October 1911 in a 13-8 win over Broughton Rangers. Papakura was the first Maori to play rugby league in Great Britain – a trailblazer and many have since followed in those footsteps.

But after his one and only first grade appearance, Papakura played for the Reserve team so chose to return to the Festival of Empire in London.

The local football team, Crystal Palace, play at nearby Selhurst Park. The team was formed by workers at the palace buildings.

Sadly, the Crystal Palace building was destroyed by a fire on 30 November 1936. But the name has continued. The area is still known as Crystal Palace and Crystal Palace Park is where the building used to be.

Between 1895 and 1914 Crystal Palace Stadium hosted the FA Cup Final. Aston Villa was the most successful club during this period as they won the Cup four times. The military required the stadium from the start of World War One and the final never returned to the stadium.

The All Blacks played their first Test match against England at Crystal Palace Stadium on the 1905 tour; 45,000 people attended the first ever Test between the All Blacks and England. It was a historic day as the Prince of Wales and other members of the royal family were in attendance. It was a record breaking day as New Zealand won 15-0 with Duncan McGregor scoring four tries – a record not equalled until Zinzan Brooke dotted down four times against Japan in 1987.

Today the park is the premier venue in London for athletics. The annual Grand Prix event takes place during the summer.

Empire Pool

Venue no longer exists:
Approximate Address: Wembley Stadium Complex, Empire Way,
London, HA9 0DW

This indoor swimming pool complex was built in 1934 and was a wonder of design for the day. It was built for the Empire Games of that year and in 1948 it was here the Olympic swimming and diving events took place. The pool was 66 yards long so to create the Olympic length a racing bridge was constructed exactly 50 metres from the deep end.

Swimming was one of the most popular events at the Olympics – both with spectators as the tickets were sold out months beforehand – and with newspaper editors who were eager to woo readers with images of scantily clad female competitors. All in the name of sport.

To give a flavour of the time, the wartime blackout paint had to be scraped off the glass ceiling to aid filming.

In 1948, Americans excelled in both swimming and diving. USA won 12 of the 16 gold medals in swimming. Their domination in diving was even more emphatic. Of the four diving events Americans claimed all the medals in two of the events and first and second in the other two events.

New Zealand's sole woman competitor in 1948 was 22-year-old Ngaire Lane. Her build up was hampered on the five-week boat trip to London where she only had a seawater filled oblong box in which to train. As it was only a foot longer than Lane, all she could do was lie on her back and kick. Upon her arrival in London, things did not get much better. She trained at the Vauxhall pool alongside the public who were more interested in bobbing about than swimming lengths. Lane eventually finished seventh in her semi-final.

Once the swimming and diving events were complete, the builders came in to construct a bridge across the pool for the boxing ring. The water beneath the ring added a strong lustre to the scene. Sir Eugene Millington-Drake of the Organising Committee wrote: 'In the evening the bright lights and many coloured flags presented a kaleidoscopic reflection in the water around the ring and without doubt enhanced the splendour of the scene.'

There were 230 fights and only one involved a New Zealander. Bob Goslin was a bantamweight when he got on the boat in Auckland – by the time he arrived in London some five weeks later – he had to move up a weight class to featherweight and he was well beaten by American Edward Johnson.

The Empire Pool had also hosted the swimming events at the 1934 British Empire Games. New Zealand's Noel Crump won a bronze medal in the Men's 100-yard freestyle.

Empress Hall

Venue no longer exists
Approximate Address: Earls Court Exhibition Centre,
Warwick Road, London, SW5 9TA

This hall in West London (across the street from Olympia Hall) was home to the Wrestling and Weightlifting musclemen at the 1948 London Olympics.

An ice rink needed to be removed prior to the start of the games. Taking place so soon after World War Two and nicknamed the Austerity Games, London even had to borrow the wrestling mats from Sweden.

The Turkish side were the strongest competitors. The team won six gold and four silver medals. The hall will have felt sparse for the competitors – there were generally only around 300 spectators watching at any time in the 8,000 seat venue.

Many of the competitors at the 1948 Olympics were war veterans. Great Britain's Jim Halliday was one such competitor at the weightlifting. He fought at Dunkirk in 1940, was captured in Japan in 1942 and upon release three years later weighed just 28kg. Halliday then regained his strength in part by eating whole eggs – shell and all. By 1947 he was the lightweight British Weightlifting Champion and he won a bronze medal at the 1948 Olympics at Empress Hall.

Another former war veteran was New Zealand weightlifter Jim Crow. From 1943 to 1946 he was with the Air Force and did not train at all. Crow put on so much weight on the five-week journey from New Zealand to London he almost had to compete as a featherweight rather than as a bantamweight. Crow eventually finished in eighth place.

Hurlingham Club, London

Ranelagh Gardens, London, SW6 3PR
www.hurlinghamclub.org.uk

There are few places in London as impressive as The Hurlingham Club.

The Club describes itself as a 'green oasis of tradition and international renown' and is set in 42 acres beside the River Thames in Fulham. There is an eight-year waiting list to join as an associate, and another eight years to become a full member.

Historically, this was an Olympic venue in 1908, when Polo was played on the grounds. Today, the British governing body of the sport is still known as the Hurlingham Polo Association, even though Polo has not been played at the club since before World War Two.

It is for croquet that the gates are occasionally opened to New Zealanders as the highly manicured croquet lawns are the home of croquet in the UK.

The Hurlingham Club hosted the first three World Association Croquet Championships from 1989 to 1991 and was again the venue in 2001.

In 1989, New Zealand's Joe Hogan became the sport's first ever World Champion when he defeated Mark Avery in the final.

Compared to Association Croquet, Golf Croquet is a more simple game to play and is growing in popularity. In 2011, the World Golf Croquet Championships took place at The Hurlingham Club and Ireland's Mark McInerney won the title while New Zealand's best-placed finisher Hamish McIntosh lost in the semi-final.

Kia Oval

Kennington, London, SE11 5SS
www.kiaoval.com

The first ground in England to host Test cricket, The Kia Oval is in South London and generally hosts England's last cricketing Test match of the summer.

The local Underground Tube station Oval, is named after the cricket ground and the station is decorated with tiled images of cricketers.

For sponsorship reasons, the ground is currently known as The Kia Oval. It has previously been known as the Brit Oval, Fosters Oval, and AMP Oval. But most sports fans have always referred to it solely as The Oval.

England played so poorly in the 1882 Test match against Australia at the Oval, losing in just two days, that the Sporting Life newspaper printed a mock obituary – which led to the creation of the Ashes.

New Zealand has played England in nine Test cricket matches at the Kia Oval. England has won four times, there have been four draws but in the most recent encounter at The Oval on the 1999 tour, New Zealand claimed the honours.

In that match in 1999, Man of the Match Chris Cairns took five wickets in the first innings and then scored a heroic 80 to give New Zealand a chance. England were dismissed for 162 – well short of the target and this was a cue for the New Zealand celebrations.

A poor England side dropped to last place on the world rankings and on the last day of the Test, the crowd chanted in mock humour: 'We've got the worst team in the world.'

In the one-day game, New Zealand lost to England in the opening game of the 1983 Cricket World Cup group match at The Kia Oval.

In a more successful match, New Zealand played USA in an ICC Champions Trophy match in 2004. This was the USA's debut in international one-day cricket. It was a difficult start for The Eagles and a record breaking day as Craig McMillan twice scored 27 runs off an over and Nathan Astle scored 145 in New Zealand's total of 347. USA was then dismissed for 137 as Jacob Oram took five wickets.

The Black Caps will return to The Kia Oval to play one-day matches against England on both their 2013 and 2015 tours.

The Kia Oval is the cricketing home of Surrey in the County Championship. Surrey is the second most successful county, behind Yorkshire, having won the County Championship 18 times. Former New Zealand captain and coach, Geoff Howarth, played for 13 years for Surrey and is the only non-English player to captain the club.

As well as cricket, The Kia Oval is famous as the home of the first ever FA

Cup final in 1872 when The Wanderers from London beat the Royal Engineers 1-0. From 1874, the ground hosted each final until 1892.

The ground is also where England played their first ever international rugby match on home soil. England lost to Scotland in 1872 by two goals to one. This was the return fixture from the first ever test match at Raeburn Place in December 1871.

Loftus Road

South Africa Road, London, W12 7PJ
www.qpr.co.uk

In West London, this is the home ground of English football side, Queen's Park Rangers. The club are known as the hoops for their blue and white hooped jerseys.

With a capacity of fewer than 19,000 it is one of the smallest grounds of the Premier League teams.

Queen's Park Rangers have been playing on and off at Loftus Road since 1917 – and prior to this, the club had played at more than 15 different grounds after it was formed in 1882.

Queen's Park Rangers reached the FA Cup in 1982 but lost to Tottenham Hotspur in a replay. The club has never won the League – their best finish was as runners up in the 1975-76 season.

In July 2012 New Zealand's Ryan Nelsen signed with the club, reuniting with his former Blackburn manager Mark Hughes.

London Wasps called the Loft home for seven years up to 2002 while Fulham ground-shared with QPR after this until 2004 while Craven Cottage was redeveloped.

The ground has been used by Australia and Jamaica to host international matches.

The Kiwis have played twice on the ground as part of the Rugby League Tri-Nations. In 2004 New Zealand lost to Australia 32-16 but a year later beat Great Britain 42-26.

London Marathon

The London Marathon takes place in the nation's capital in March or April around the River Thames.

The race currently starts at Blackheath and after 26 gruelling miles, competitors cross the finish line on the Mall in sight of Buckingham Palace.

The Marathon was created by former Olympic athletes John Disley and the late Chris Brasher – inspired by the New York Marathon. The first race was in 1981 and with almost 8,000 competitors. American Dick Beardsley and Norway's Inge Simonsen staged a dead heat finish for the Men's race. Joyce Hill broke the British record to win the Women's race.

Hundreds of thousands of spectators line the streets to cheer on the competitors – many dressed in quite unbelievable costumes in order to raise money for charity. It has been estimated that over £500 million has been raised in total. 2007 was a world record for a single annual fundraising event – £46.7 million.

Some of the famous charity runners have included Lloyd Scott who completed the 2002 marathon wearing a deep-sea diving suit that weighed more than 50kg. His time was 5 days 8 hours plus.

Other outrageous costumes have included a 7 metre high giraffe and a rhinoceros.

In 2010 Princess Beatrice became the first royal to complete the London Marathon. What's more she was part of a 34 strong 'human caterpillar' team – all tied together with bungee cords.

No New Zealander has ever won the Marathon but many, many New Zealanders have taken part – either as Marathon visitors or while living in the UK.

New Zealand women competed at the highest level in the early 1980s. Gillian Drake finished second in 1981 as did Lorraine Moller in 1982 as well as Mary O'Connor in 1983 and 1986. Judith Hines finished third behind Moller in 1982.

More recently, in 2010, Kim Smith broke the New Zealand marathon record at London finishing in a time of 2:25:21.

Lord's

St John's Wood, London, NW8 8QN
www.lords.org

The home of cricket. There are certain sports grounds that you go to, but going to Lord's as a cricket fan, you will feel like you've arrived.

They have been playing cricket here in North London on this site for almost 200 years. This ground was named after its founder Thomas Lord – so the name is Lord's not Lords. It is actually the third ground Lord established, but the first two have long since been abandoned.

The Pavilion (and the well-known Long Room within it) is the most famous stand within the ground. It is primarily for members of Marylebone Cricket Club (MCC) but it also houses the players' dressing rooms and the players' balcony. Within the dressing rooms are the honours boards on which a player's name is inscribed if they make a test century or take five wickets in a test innings.

The Long Room is exclusively for members of the MCC and tradition dictates, all members must wear a jacket and tie.

The ground is surprisingly sloped and this can create movement and variable bounce off the pitch. The nursery pitch beside the main pitch also hosts cricket matches.

From wherever you sit at Lord's, the imposing Media Centre building looms over you. While it looks more like a space ship that has fallen to earth, it is actually home to the journalists and television presenters who comment on the game.

Lord's is also home to a wonderful cricketing museum, which includes sporting memorabilia that is world class. It is home to The Ashes, cricketing attire from years gone by and there is even a stuffed sparrow.

New Zealand played their first Test match on British soil against England at Lord's in 1931. This match ended in a draw as did the next matches in 1937 and 1949.

The 1949 match is memorable for Martin Donnelly's double century – he is still the only New Zealander to achieve this at the ground and one of only seven non-Englishmen to ever reach 200 at Lord's.

Since that first match in 1931, New Zealand has lost to England six times and there have been eight draws in total.

But in 1999 New Zealand recorded their first and only victory at the home of cricket. Chris Cairns took six wickets, Matt Horne made a century and when England could only make 229 in their second innings, New Zealand needed just 58 runs. Matthew Bell scored the winning runs and New Zealand celebrated their first ever win at Lords after 68 years of trying.

Lord's was also the venue for archery during the 2012 London Olympics.

As well as hosting four World Cup one-day finals – in 1975, 79, 83 and 99, Lord's also staged the final of the Women's World Cup in 1993 when New Zealand lost to England.

If you are visiting on a non-match day, the Lord's Tavern is a popular spot for a drink or a meal and it is open throughout the year. Enter the home of cricket through the Grace Gate.

But on a match day, The Duke of York Pub, in the heart of St John's Wood, is a great place for a drink or a meal at the end of play.

New Zealand Batsmen on the Honours Board at Lord's;	New Zealand Bowlers on the Honours Board at Lord's;
Jacob Oram	Daniel Vettori
Mark Richardson	Chris Cairns
Matt Horne	Dion Nash
Martin Crowe	Richard Hadlee
Trevor Franklin	
Geoff Howarth	
Bevan Congdon	
Mark Burgess	
Vic Pollard	
Martin Donnelly	
Stewie Dempster	
Milton 'Curly' Page	

Queen Elizabeth Olympic Park

Loop Road, Stratford, London, E20 2ST

Queen Elizabeth Olympic Park encompasses many of the venues that were used as part of the 2012 London Olympics.

The Park will open in stages during 2013 and 2014.

The Olympic Stadium was the focal point of the 2012 London Olympics and Paralympics. The Opening and Closing Ceremonies were held at the Stadium as was the athletics competition.

New Zealand's Valerie Adams won a gold medal in the Women's Shot Put. She finished second behind Nadzeya Ostapchuk on the night but was promoted after the Belarusian was disqualified for failing a drugs test.

As well as the stadium, the Park is home to the Velodrome, the Aquatic Centre and the Riverbank Arena.

At the Velodrome during the Olympics, New Zealand's Team Pursuit won a bronze medal as did Simon van Velthooven in the Men's Keiren.

Phillipa Grey with her pilot Laura Thompson won a gold medal on the track in the Women's Individual Pursuit in the Paralympics.

New Zealanders excelled at the Aquatics Centre during the Paralympics. Sophie Pascoe won three gold and three silver medals in the pool while Cameron Leslie and Mary Fisher also won their events.

The Queen's Club

Palliser Road, London, W14 9EQ
www.queensclub.co.uk

When the United Kingdom was a great power in the world and London was at its centre, it was The Queen's Club (Queen's) where tennis' great and good came to play.

The private sporting club was founded in 1886 and named after its first patron Queen Victoria. The club was the host of 'Real Tennis' when London hosted the Olympics in 1908.

The Queen's Club clubhouse.

It annually hosts the Queen's Championships in June on its beautifully kept grass courts and the tournament is one of the lead-up events to Wimbledon.

New Zealand's Anthony Wilding won the tournament at Queen's four times – firstly in 1907 and then three consecutive titles from 1910 to 1912. Compatriot, Harry Parker made the final in 1909 but lost to 1908 Olympic champion Major Josiah Ritchie in the final.

It was Major Ritchie who Anthony Wilding beat in the finals in 1910 and 1911. They had previously teamed up together in 1908 and 1910 to win the Men's Doubles at Wimbledon. Interestingly, Ritchie was not a military man – his first name actually was Major.

The British Covered Court Championship was played annually at Queen's from 1890 right up until 1971. Anthony Wilding won the Men's event here in 1907.

The World Covered Court Championships were established in 1913 as part of a series of World Championship events and in 1920 Queen's Club was host. That year, former New Zealand MP Francis Fisher teamed up with South African Irene Peacock to win the Mixed Doubles and lost in the final of the Men's Doubles.

More recently, Andy Murray captured his second Queen's title in 2011 and the event is a highlight of the British sporting and social calendar.

River Thames

The river that snakes its way through London starts as a small culvert high in the Cotswold hills about 215 miles away.

The river has traditionally been an economic motorway to move goods, a geographic border, a place to play and an area of great tourism as the boat trip visitors and riverside businesses will testify.

From a sporting viewpoint, the river is most famous for its rowing. There are over 200 rowing clubs based along the river.

The Oxford versus Cambridge Boat race is one of the year's sporting highlights. It takes place each spring – on the last Saturday of March or the first Saturday in April. The race currently takes place from Putney to Mortlake but when the race began in 1829, it took place in Henley on Thames, racing from Hambledon Lock to Henley Bridge. The second race took place in 1836 when the race went from Westminster to Putney. The first race on the current course took place in 1843.

There was no New Zealander in that first race in 1829, but George Selwyn, a man important to the future of New Zealand, rowed for Cambridge that year. He became the first Anglican Bishop of New Zealand, and many parts of New Zealand bear his name – Selwyn College in Otago, the Selwyn River in Canterbury, the Selwyn electorate, Selwyn Road in the Bay of Islands and Selwyn House at Kings College, Auckland among many others.

His son, John Richardson Selwyn was born in the Bay of Islands. He became the first New Zealand born rower in the boat race when he went to the UK to attend Eton and then Cambridge. He was on the losing side in 1864 and again in 1866.

New Zealand's H.D. Gillies in 1904 raced on the winning side for Cambridge as did Scott Brownlee in 1995. In 2009, Olympic medallist, George Bridgewater was a winner for Oxford.

New Zealand has supplied numerous coaches to both sides. Esteemed coach Harry Mahon led the Cambridge team to nine wins out of 10 attempts between 1993 and 2001. Chris Nilsson and Duncan Holland have also coached the teams in the past years.

Like the Boat Race, The Henley Royal Regatta in July is viewed by some as an important rowing festival, but with a party going on beside. Others view the five-day Regatta as an important occasion on the social calendar with rowing taking place in the background. It is a great day for a straw hat and a jug of Pimms.

The Royal Regatta was first held in 1839. The Grand Challenge Cup is for the eights, and the Stewards' Challenge Cup is for fours.

Since the turn of the millennium, New Zealanders have competed with great aplomb at the Regatta. Mahé Drysdale is a three-times winner while Eric Murray and Hamish Bond have twice won the Silver Goblets and Nickalls Challenge Cup for the Pairs. Murray and Bond were following in the footsteps of John Selwyn who won the same race in 1864.

Henley is different to most rowing festivals in that it operates a knockout system rather than a multi-lane system.

Royal Agricultural Hall

52 Upper Street, London, N1 0QH

The Royal Agricultural Hall seems an unlikely venue for the site of one of New Zealand's finest earliest sporting moments.

In the late 1800s Pedestrianism was a hugely popular spectator sport with thousands of spectators cramming into stadiums to watch the stars of the day.

The sport developed from walking matches – often for the purpose of the public betting on two athletes who aimed to cover enormous distances by foot.

The earliest hero was Edward Watson who walked 100 miles in under 23 hours and 500 miles over six days. Races tended to be a maximum of six days because in Victorian times, Sunday was always a day of rest. In 1877 Weston took on Daniel O'Leary in the UK and 70,000 were in attendance.

British MP Sir John Astley was enamoured with the sport and created a six day 'Long Distance Challenge Championship of the World'. The international version and an English version in which competitors raced over six days for 144 hours or 72 hours respectively.

The sport was also popular in New Zealand and Australia. Dunedin's Joe Scott won the NZ Championship in 1879 at Garrison Hall. In 1885 Scott set the 100-mile world record (17 hours 59 minutes) and in 1886 he became the Australian National Champion.

Joe Scott then travelled to the UK to compete for the 1888 Astley Belt.

Scott won warm up races at the London Royal Aquarium and then competed for the Belt at the Agricultural Hall in Islington, north London. Six days of walking – 12 hours each day. Scott took the lead on the fourth day and eventually won the race with 363 miles 1,510 yards in 71 hours, 51 minutes while Jack Hibberd finished second with 337 miles.

Scott's winning distance is the equivalent of walking from Oamaru to Blenheim or from Auckland to Taupo and then turning round and going back to Auckland.

There is historical debate as to whether Scott won £100 or £200 for his efforts but there is no doubt about the hero's welcome he received upon his return to New Zealand.

By the turn of the century, popularity in pedestrianism had begun to wane, but the sport was a forerunner to race walking – which has been part of the Olympics since 1908. That same year Joe Scott died and he was inducted into the New Zealand Sports Hall of Fame in 1995.

Today, the Royal Agricultural Hall has become the Business Design Centre – which hosts conferences and exhibitions.

Royal Albert Hall

Kensington Gore, London, SW7 2AP
www.royalalberthall.com

Situated in the upmarket district of Kensington & Chelsea this grand old concert hall is a British treasure and a visit there is a treat. Sitting opposite Hyde Park, it is affectionately known both as 'the Nation's Hall' and as 'the World's most famous stage.'

The Royal Albert Hall opened in 1871 and today it is most famous for hosting the annual BBC Promenade Concerts (the Proms). This series of classical orchestral concerts held throughout the summer attracts an audience who do not normally attend classical music concerts.

But the BBC Proms are one of many concerts that take place at the Hall each year. Pop bands love to play at the Royal Albert Hall for the acoustics and often record their DVDs 'Live at the Albert Hall'.

In 1963 the Beatles and Rolling Stones both played on the same bill. Led Zeppelin, The Who, Jimi Hendrix, Frank Sinatra, Ella Fitzgerald, Pavarotti, Elton John, Eric Clapton, Robbie Williams, Bob Dylan and Jay-Z are among the many stars to have taken to the Royal Albert Hall stage.

On a classical front, Wagner, Verdi and Elgar all made their first UK performances here. New Zealand's Dame Kiri Te Kanawa celebrated her 50th birthday at the Hall in 1994 with a spectacular birthday concert.

When the hall was built, the organ was one of the centrepieces and at the time it was the largest in the world. When the organ was refurbished and restored in 2004, it was Dame Gillian Weir who was one of the first to perform on it. Weir was born in New Zealand in 1941 and moved to the UK in her 20s and has gone on to become a world-renowned concert organist.

The Royal Albert Hall has hosted events ranging from Ballet to Miss World beauty pageants, Car shows to film premiers, internationals speakers and a Harry Potter book launch.

On a sporting front basketball, wrestling, table tennis and sumo wrestling have all taken place at the Hall. Tennis has been played at the Royal Albert Hall since the 1970s and this continues today as heroes from yesteryear fill the Hall each December in the Masters series. The 1987 World Squash Open was also held here.

In the past, major boxing nights were staged at the Hall. Infamously, notorious gangland criminal brothers Ronnie, Reggie and Charlie Kray all boxed here on the same night in December 1951.

It was here that New Zealand's Bos Murphy won the British Empire Middleweight title in 1948 by beating Vince Hawkins over 15 rounds. In doing so he became the first New Zealander to win a British Empire title.

Murphy ended up in the UK after fleeing his homeland. His New Zealand boxing license was revoked in 1947 because he allegedly knew that Willie Jones had taken a dive in their fight.

It was a heavy fall from grace for Murphy because only a year earlier he had been the darling of the New Zealand public. He had beaten Australian Vic Patrick in a fight that captured the nation's attention. Peter Fraser (New Zealand's Prime Minister at the time) climbed into the Petone Ring in front of 12,000 fans and said: 'We are proud of you, my boy.'

British stars such as Frank Bruno, Lennox Lewis and Joe Calzaghe have all boxed at the Hall.

Stamford Bridge

Fulham Road, London, SW6 1HS
www.chelseafc.com

The stadium dates back to the 1870s when it was built as a stadium for the London Athletics Club.

It was not until the early 1900s when Gus Mears bought the ground and created Chelsea Football Club.

The All Blacks beat Middlesex at 'The Bridge' on the 1905 tour by 34-0. On the day Auckland winger, George Smith, scored two tries. It was not Smith's first success on the ground – three years earlier he had won the AAA 120 yards hurdles (the equivalent of today's British Athletics Championships). Smith later played for the 1907 rugby league All Golds and it is rumoured but unconfirmed that he had previously won the 1894 New Zealand Cup as a jockey aboard Imperial.

Jack Lovelock was the next New Zealand speedster at Stamford Bridge as he set a world record in June 1932 for three quarters of a mile beating England's Jerry Cornes.

In the past Stamford Bridge has also hosted Greyhound racing, American football, Speedway, day-night cricket and even a baseball match between New York and Chicago in 1915, but it is for football as home to Chelsea that the ground is best known. The stadium hosted the FA Cup three times between 1920 and 1922 attracting crowds of 70,000 plus.

Chelsea have become a major force in European football but this is a recent phenomenon. The club yo-yoed between the top two divisions in its early years but the appointment of a new manager in 1952, Ted Drake, led the team to its first League title in 1955.

The 1970s and 1980s were turbulent times as the club struggled with financial crises. Chelsea were playing Second Division football in 1988.

The biggest turnaround at Chelsea happened in 2003 when Roman Abramovich bought the club. In the 'Chelski' years the club has won three League titles, four FA Cups and the crowning glory was winning the Champions League in May 2012 over Bayern Munich in a dramatic final.

Chelsea's success on the pitch may have implications for Stamford Bridge. While the club wishes to expand capacity, there are numerous constraints such as two railway lines, a main road and the stadium's location in a busy part of west London. The club is considering moving but many fans do not want to leave their famous home.

Visitors can learn more about the club and the stadium at the on-site museum.

From a historical point of view, the best place for a drink before the game is at The Butchers Hook (previously called The Rising Sun), which is where the club was first formed.

Thurston's Hall

Venue no longer exists
Approximate Address: Leicester Square, London, WC2

In Leicester Square in London, this snooker hall was the home of the World Snooker Championships from its inception in 1927 to the post war period. It was named after Thurston – the famous Billiard and Snooker Table manufacturer.

The hall was an intimate venue with seating for about 220. The famed snooker commentator Clive Everton visited the Hall as a child and described it as being 'like a small cathedral, except for the cigar smoke'.

In 1932, from 25 April to 30 April, New Zealand's Clark McConachy battled England's Joe Davis over 49 frames. Unlike today, they played all 49 frames even though the match result was known after 43 frames when Davis won the clinching frame to take an unassailable 25-18 lead. The match finished 30 frames to 19.

This was Davis' sixth consecutive World Championship title. He remained the only winner of the tournament he conceived from 1927 and he would win every year up until 1940 – when the tournament was postponed until after the war. Upon resumption in 1946 Joe Davis won again before his brother Fred Davis won the next three titles.

In 1951 the Hall had been renamed as the Leicester Square Hall and was the site of the World Billiard Championship. Clark McConachy beat John Barrie by 9,294 to 6,691. McConachy scored the highest break with a 481. In a report of the game, 'McConachy gave an exhibition of magical billiards, excelling in all phases of the game … The lover of the art will treasure McConachy's display as an unforgettable display of the art and poetry of the game.'

In January 1955 at Leicester Square Hall, Joe Davis finally made the very first official maximum snooker break of 147 – all 15 reds and blacks, followed by the seven colours. The match was an exhibition to celebrate the closure of the great Snooker and Billiards Hall and the building was demolished in 1956.

Today, Leicester Square is still one of London's centres of entertainment. There are nightclubs and theatres and the Odeon Cinema often hosts world premiers of major movies – such as the Harry Potter series. Thurston's Hall would have been approximately sited where All Bar One is now.

In Leicester Square, you can find various pavement squares, which have distances to all of the countries which were formerly in the British Empire. Wellington is 11,689 miles away!

Twickenham

200 Whitton Road, Twickenham, Middlesex, TW2 7BA
www.rfu.com

The name immediately conjures up images for rugby fans. If it's the 32-6 thrashing in 2008 on the end of season tour or the heartbreaking loss to France in the 1999 World Cup, Twickers is the headquarters of English rugby.

Before the ground was built, the area was a cabbage patch and England hosted its first international against Wales in 1910. The English RFU had seen the financial benefits of owning their own ground after the All Blacks match with England at Crystal Palace in 1905 was a sell out.

Since the All Blacks first match in 1924 (a 17-11 victory), New Zealand have played England another 17 times on the ground. In total 13 wins, four losses and a 26-26 draw in 1997.

As well as that quarter-final loss to France, the All Blacks have also played London Counties, Combined Services, London and South-East and more recently the Barbarians on the ground.

After redevelopments through the early part of this century, the stadium currently holds 82,000 fans and is the largest stadium dedicated to rugby in the world.

As well as All Black games, you can watch the British leg of the World Sevens Series at Twickenham. It's one more chance to cheer on New Zealanders beating England. The stadium has previously hosted the opening game of the Rugby League World Cup in 2000 and Challenge Cup Finals while Wembley Stadium was being renovated. The rugby Premiership final takes place in May while the annual Oxford versus Cambridge University match is in December.

The stadium is home to the World Rugby Museum, which is an interactive, hands-on museum with a great collection of rugby photos and memorabilia.

One of the most famous visitors to Twickenham was Erica Roe – who became the first streaker across the pitch in 1982 during an England versus Australia match. England captain Bill Beaumont was giving his half-time speech on the pitch but noticed little concentration from his team. He said later: 'I was trying to get through to the boys, but most of them seemed to be gazing over my shoulder.' Annoyed, he turned around and he then understood why as Erika Roe ran towards him, chased by security guards. The half-time speech was over.

On game days, and especially for All Black matches, it's always good to have a drink at one of the many riverside pubs before the game. Favourites are The London Apprentice and The Barmy Arms.

You could also try the aptly named Cabbage Patch or the William Webb Ellis which are both great pubs but do get very busy before and after the game. The banter between opposing fans is traditionally very good and for rugby fans a match at Twickenham is a very special occasion.

Twickenham Stoop

Langhorn Drive, Twickenham, Middlesex, TW2 7SX
www.quins.co.uk

Situated near to its big brother, Twickenham, the Stoop is a smaller rugby ground where New Zealand's women won their fourth consecutive Rugby World Cup in 2010.

The team had played their preliminary group games at Surrey Sports Park in Guildford but the semi-finals and final were played at the Stoop, which holds almost 15,000 fans.

The Black Ferns beat France 45-7 in the semi-final and played England in the final. Carla Hohepa touched down in the first half and with 20 minutes to go the scores were tied at 10-10. Kelly Brazier kicked the winning penalty and New Zealand held on for a 13-10 victory. Captained by Melissa Ruscoe, this was the team's fourth World Cup victory.

On a more regular basis, Harlequins play in England's Rugby Premiership and won their first ever Premiership final in May 2012. Zinzan Brooke and Andrew Mehrtens both played for Quins when they moved to the UK.

After the World Cup in 2007, Nick Evans signed for Harlequins and his decision to then re-sign with the club made him ineligible for the 2011 World Cup winning squad.

London Broncos Rugby League are attempting to reach out to fans of the 13-a-side game in the capital but in London the game is still viewed by many as a northern game for working men.

Originally, the ground was called Stoop Memorial Ground after Adrian Stoop – a rugby player and then an administrator with the Harlequins club and president for almost 30 years.

Wembley Stadium

Wembley Stadium, Wembley, London, HA9 0WS
www.wembleystadium.com

This stadium in North London has been home to some of sport's greatest events. Challenge Cup finals, FA Cup Finals, a World Cup Rugby League Final, concerts, the Olympics, Speedway World Championships, Champions League finals, NFL matches, the 1966 World Cup Final and even the Live Aid concert in 1985.

The first Wembley Stadium was closed in 2000 and demolished in 2003 to make way for the new Wembley Stadium, which opened in 2007.

Pele described Wembley Stadium as 'the cathedral of football. It is the capital of football and it is the heart of football'.

The first match played on the ground was the FA Cup Final in 1923 between Bolton and West Ham. The FA never imagined so many people would want to come to the new stadium and while the capacity was 127,000 the estimates of people there range from 200,000 up to 300,000 people. A white horse called Billy helped to push the fans back off the pitch and the game began 45 minutes late. In honour of Billy, the footbridge outside the stadium has been named in tribute to him.

From a global perspective, the 1948 Olympics were a standout for the stadium. Fannie Blankers-Koen from The Netherlands was the starlet of the track as she won four gold medals. With two children, and aged 30, she was

The statue of England's World Cup winning captain
Bobby Moore at Wembley.

affectionately nicknamed 'The Flying Housewife'. She may have won more, but females were limited to only three individual events.

John Holland competed in the 400 metre hurdles at the Games for New Zealand. He went on to win bronze at Helsinki in the same event four years later. Harold Nelson wore the black jersey over 5,000 and 10,000 metres. Doug Harris competed in the 800 metres.

From a British viewpoint, the finest hour at Wembley Stadium came in 1966, when Geoff Hurst scored a hat-trick to win the World Cup for England on home soil, beating Germany after extra-time.

The iconic image of the old stadium was the twin towers but today it is the 133 metre tall arch above the stadium, which is the focal point.

Apart from the years when the new stadium was being built, Wembley Stadium is the home of the FA Cup Final. From the 1990s onwards it became home to the semi-finals as well.

Wembley Stadium also hosted Greyhound races. The opening meeting in 1927 attracted 50,000 people and greyhound racing continued until 1998.

The All Blacks have played once at the ground. In 1997 when the Millennium stadium was being built, New Zealand beat Wales 42-7.

Every year since 1946 (apart from the redevelopment years) generally two rugby league teams from the North of England make the trek to London to play in the Challenge Cup final.

The Lance Todd Trophy is given to the Man of the Match in the Challenge Cup. It is named in honour of New Zealand's former Wigan player, Salford Manager and BBC Commentator, Lance Todd who died in a car accident in 1942. Five New Zealanders have won the trophy including Jeff Lima for Wigan in 2011.

The Kiwis played Great Britain in the first of three Tests in 1993. The hosts ran out 17-0 victors. Jason Robinson debuted for Great Britain and scored two tries on the day.

Their first match at the new Wembley Stadium was against Wales in November 2011 as part of the Four Nations tournament double header. The Kiwis won 36-0.

In 1929, Sir Arthur Elvin (the chairman of the stadium) asked New Zealander Johnnie Hoskins to promote speedway at the stadium. He created the Wembley Lions and Hoskins is credited with being integral to the success of the sport.

The stadium hosted 24 Speedway World Championships – including all 15 finals between 1936 and 1960 and then another nine up until 1981. Of those Wembley Stadium finals, New Zealanders, Ronnie Moore, Barry Briggs and Ivan Mauger claimed victory in seven of them.

Today the stadium has a 90,000 capacity making it the second largest in Europe behind the Camp Nou in Barcelona.

Wembley Stadium also annually hosts the only regular season NFL game held outside of North America and in 2011, the Chicago Bears beat Tampa Bay 24-18.

Wembley Stadium regularly hosts major concert events – and there was none bigger than Live Aid, which was held in 1985. Organised by Bob Geldof and Midge Ure, the concert raised awareness and money for the famines in Ethiopia.

You can take a tour of Wembley Stadium today, where you can walk up the steps to the royal box and be photographed with the FA Cup, go behind the scenes, visit the dressing rooms, and see the trophies.

If you are going to the match or to tour the stadium, Wembley Park Station is the closest tube station. Walk up Olympic Way and see the statue to 1966 World Cup winning Captain Bobby Moore. If you travel to Wembley Central Station, you will walk across the White Horse Bridge.

There are 34 bars, eight restaurants and 688 food and drink service points so you will not go hungry or thirsty before or after the game.

The nearby Wembley Arena and Conference Centre also hosts major sporting events. It was here that New Zealand's Susan Devoy won the British Open Squash title every year between 1984 and 1990 and then again in 1992. The Arena also now hosts the Masters Snooker Tournament in January.

Wembley Stadium is beautiful and from a customer point of view the whole experience is wonderful. Whether your team wins or loses you are sure of a great time.

White City Stadium

Stadium no longer exists
Approximate Address: Wood Lane, London W12

Built for the 1908 Olympic Games, this major London Stadium was the venue of some of sport's great moments. In fact it has been known as The Great Stadium.

It was the main stadium for the Olympics in 1908 and for the second ever British Empire Games in 1934. It has also been the home of football club, Queen's Park Rangers, it has hosted major boxing fights and in 1966 one match at the World Cup was played at the ground. It has also been a speedway venue; the home of concerts and you could have watched greyhounds racing there.

It was viewed as the forerunner to modern stadia and while there was seating for 68,000 it could hold more than 130,000 standing on the terraces.

The 1908 Olympics were the first time New Zealanders competed – as part of the Australasia team.

France withdrew from the Rugby Union competition so as the only two teams, the Australasia team played a Great Britain team (represented by Cornwall which had won the County Championship). Australasia beat Great Britain 32-3 to win the gold.

A swimming pool was built inside the stadium on the infield and all swimming competitions took place here.

One of the more interesting events at the 1908 Games was the Tug of War. The final was contested between the Liverpool Police force and the City of London Police force with the local team pulling off the victory.

On the track, Harry Kerr wrote his name into New Zealand's sporting history as the country's first ever Olympic medallist. In the 3,500 metre walk, Kerr, from Taranaki, finished third to claim the bronze medal. New Zealand's Albert Edward MacKay Rowland, finished fifth in the race and won a diploma.

All three New Zealanders competed on the track in 1908 because Henry Murray, from Christchurch, competed in the 110 metre hurdles and 400 metre hurdles. Murray also carried the flag for Australasia. A fourth New Zealander, Arthur Halligan, from Dannevirke, competed for Great Britain in the 110 metre hurdles, finished second in his heat but did not progress to the final.

In 1934 White City was the host of the British Empire Games where Jack Lovelock was the hero winning the Men's Mile. Lovelock, who captained the New Zealand side, had been in the UK since 1931 when he arrived to study at Oxford on a Rhodes scholarship. Harold Brainsby won a bronze medal in the Triple Jump and finished seventh in the Long Jump.

Lovelock famously went on to win the gold medal in the 1,500 metres at the Berlin Olympics in 1936. Soon after the games, a match between the USA and the British Empire was held at White City. Lovelock was part of the winning three-mile team race but USA beat the Empire 5-3. This was Lovelock's last ever race on British soil.

Queen's Park Rangers spent two separate spells at White City. The team moved from Loftus Road for the 1931-32 season and a record crowd of over 41,000 watched them beat Leeds but the team returned to Loftus Road two years later having made financial losses.

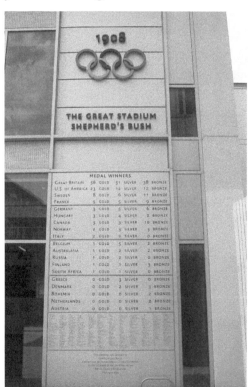

The financial lesson was not learned. For half of the 1962-63 season, QPR again played at White City but returned to Loftus Road as attendances were not as high as expected.

White City was also a speedway venue and between 1976 and 1978 it was home to the White City Rebels. Even though the Rebels won the championship in 1977 the team was disbanded just a year later due to poor crowds.

In 1979 White City played host to the Speedway World Cup and

The memorial to White City Stadium where the 1908 Olympics took place.

the New Zealand team of Larry Ross, Mitch Shirra, Ivan Mauger and Bruce Cribb won. This is the only time New Zealand won the World Cup although a number of Kiwis including Mauger as well as Barry Briggs and Ronnie Moore were part of previously successful Great Britain teams.

The stadium was demolished in 1985 to make way for the BBC buildings.

Willesden Sports Centre

Donnington Road, Willesden, London, NW10 3QX

In suburban north-west London, a not very impressive sports stadium was transformed into the home of the Men's Hockey World Cup in October 1986. The tournament was awarded to England as it was 100 years since the formation of the Hockey Association in 1886.

It was the first World Cup to be played on an artificial surface. New Zealand was drawn with the Netherlands, Pakistan, USSR, Argentina and hosts England.

At the group stage, New Zealand lost four out of its five group games, drawing only against Argentina.

In the Play-off games, the Black Sticks beat India and then Canada to finish in ninth place.

In the final Australia beat England 2-1. Mark Hager won gold with the Australian team and was appointed coach of the New Zealand women's side in 2008.

Wimbledon

Church Road, Wimbledon, London, SW19 5AE
www.wimbledon.com

On a sporting tour of the UK, Wimbledon is among the most famous venues.

In New Zealand, tennis is very accessible to people, and Wimbledon is the most iconic tennis club in the world. The All England Championships at Wimbledon is a wonderful event to visit as a spectator.

The two-week tournament manages to combine everything that is traditionally British – great expectations on the leading local player, queuing, history, a drink, pride in being British, rain delays, royalty and eventual disappointment when the home player loses in the semi-final.

A glass of Pimms, a punnet of strawberries and a ticket to Wimbledon's centre-court is as good as life gets for a tennis fan.

The championship celebrated 125 years in 2011. The All England Lawn Tennis and Croquet Club was founded in 1868 and the tournament started in 1877 at Worple Road. The tournament moved to its current site in 1922. Originally, the tournament was strictly for Gentlemen – the first Ladies Singles tournament was in 1884.

It was at Worple Road, that legendary New Zealander, Anthony Wilding won the title four consecutive times between 1910 and 1913 and lost in the final the following year. He also collected four doubles titles in this time. War intervened and Wilding died in action in northern France in 1915.

In 1983 Chris Lewis became the first New Zealander to make the semi-finals since Wilding. His five-set victory over South African Kevin Curren is considered one of the great Wimbledon matches. He was an outsider, ranked number 91 in the world, was up against the World number 12, who had just beaten Jimmy Connors. In the match of the tournament, Lewis won 8-6 in the fifth set. Lewis was a sensation and one paper exclaimed 'Hail Mr Nobody'.

In an interview for TVNZ, Lewis said he remembers '…every match as if it was yesterday, it is very, very vivid in my mind.' When asked to nominate three special memories, he said: 'Stepping out to serve for the match in the fifth, four points away from the final, Curren hitting that backhand wide on match point and walking out on the court for the final.'

Up against John McEnroe, he was beaten easily. In that same interview he described the fiery American as '…too good and there was nothing I could really do to stop it'. Today, Lewis runs tennis-experts.com from his Californian base.

Chris Lewis had previously tasted success at Wimbledon after he won the Boys' final in 1975 as an 18-year-old. Brian Fairlie had been runner-up in the Boys' event in 1966. Elizabeth Terry was in the final of the Girls event in 1962 as was Julie Richardson in 1985 in the Girls Doubles' final.

Steven Downs and James Greenhalgh went one better when they won the Boys' Doubles in 1993.

Aorangi Terrace – Spectators watching the big screen from 'The Hill' during Wimbledon 2012.

Aorangi Terrace – signposted at Wimbledon.

Marina Erakovic and her partner lost in the Girls' Doubles final in 2004 and 2005 and in 2011 Erakovic lost in the semi-finals of the Women's Doubles. With her partner Tamarin Tanasugarn they had made it all the way through the qualifying stages. They were lucky to get through as they lost a qualifying match but advanced as 'lucky losers' after another pair were forced to pull out.

Onny Parun reached the men's quarter-finals in 1971 and 1972. He described the experience as 'probably every tennis player's dream to play there and when you get there it is probably better than you even imagine'.

Ruia Morrison became the first Maori to play at Wimbledon in 1957 and reached the quarter-finals. She played again at Wimbledon until 1960.

The Museum at Wimbledon is a goldmine for any tennis fan. Everything from the trophies, racquets and balls from yesteryear, fashion, memorabilia, and much more are on display.

If you are in England at anytime when The Championship is not on, you can do a guided tour and visit the Museum as well as go behind the scenes. You can step onto Centre Court and see behind the scenes to what goes on at the most well known tennis courts in the world.

But the best time to visit Wimbledon is during the tournament. Tickets for Centre Court and Number One court are difficult to obtain. You can apply for tickets in the ballot a year in advance, or during the first nine days of the tournament you can queue overnight for one of the tickets issued each day. The traditional British queue starts up to two days before so bring a sleeping bag and provisions.

While the most popular players are on the two centre courts, there is tennis played on 20 courts throughout the tournament so by paying the ground admission (costing between £15 and £20 in 2012), you are certain to have an enjoyable day. For many people, the best matches are those that you stumble upon on the outside courts. There are often fewer than 100 of you watching two of the best players in the world.

You can easily while away an afternoon watching the tennis on the big screen from Aorangi Terrace. While it may be known to many fans as 'Henman Hill' or 'Murray Mountain', it was named in honour of New Zealand's Mount Cook as the land was previously leased to the New Zealand Sports and Social Club.

Top tip: On Final's weekend get in the queue for returned tickets after the Men's and Women's Singles' finals. Many corporate ticket holders only want to see the Singles' finals and do not want to watch the Doubles' finals. For less than £10 you can buy one of these returned tickets and watch a Doubles final on Centre Court. In the past 10 years you could have seen Martina Navritilova, Kim Clijsters, Amelie Mauresmo and Serena and Venus Williams – all major champion winners.

Wimbledon Greyhound Stadium (Plough Lane)

Wimbledon Greyhound Stadium, Plough Lane, Wimbledon, SW17 OBL
www.lovethedogs.co.uk

In the 1950s, 60s and 70s it was New Zealanders who dominated the world of Speedway. World Championships and team championships were generally won by men from down under.

The birth of this success came at Plough Lane as the Wimbledon Dons Speedway teams dominated the sport with New Zealanders leading the way. Between 1954 and 1961 Wimbledon Dons won seven out of the eight National Leagues.

The trio of Christchurch riders synonymous with speedway all had spells at Plough Lane. Ivan Mauger's first two years in British speedway were with Wimbledon – starting as a 16-year-old in 1956. He was joining the other two members of New Zealand's great Speedway triumvirate. It was Ronnie Moore who inspired him to take up Speedway and Mauger worked as an assistant on the track in between practising. He cleaned the toilets, weeded the gardens and learnt everything he could from Ronnie.

Ronnie Moore spent 13 years with Wimbledon between 1950 and 1963. He was Speedway World Champion in 1954 and 1959. He returned to the club in 1969 for another three years and became World Pairs Champion with Ivan Mauger in 1970.

The third member of Speedway's grand triumvirate, Barry Briggs, joined Wimbledon in 1952 and spent seven years at the club before moving across London to join New Cross Rangers. While at Plough Lane he won the World Championship in 1957 and 1958.

Geoff Mardon was also at the club in the early 1950s. Larry Ross raced for the Dons in the late 1970s but by this time the club's star was beginning to fade and Speedway's popularity in London was beginning to decline.

The decline was slow through the 1980s and the club eventually closed in 1991. The club made a brief comeback in 2002, but the team quickly folded. The team could not afford the rent charged by the owners of the stadium.

Today the stadium is occasionally used for motor racing events such as Stock Cars but the primary use is Greyhound racing. The English Derby is the most prestigious race of the Greyhound year and has been staged on the track since 1985. The track hosts racing every Friday and Saturday night.

South East England

For the purposes of this book, the South East covers a wide area – from Hampshire across the south coast up to Norfolk, Cambridgeshire and down through Oxfordshire.

It's a wide and diverse region with so many sporting venues, travel highlights and areas of historical and cultural significance. So for each ceremonial county here is a highlight or two but travel without bounds means discovering your own England.

Hampshire and The Isle of Wight: The naval strongholds of Portsmouth and Southampton are bitter rivals on the football pitch but both towns are fascinating to visit and gain an insight into why Britain previously ruled the waves. Take the ferry from either town to visit the Isle of Wight.

West Sussex: More than its seaside resorts, West Sussex is home to motor racing and horse racing at Goodwood. If you're hunting for British sunshine, you've found it as 1,900 hours per year gives it more sunshine than any other county in the UK.

East Sussex: A trip to the Brighton seaside is a quintessentially English day out. Walk along the pier; look out to sea and dream of the beaches back home. Consider how built up British beaches are with arcades, fairs and stalls and how noisy they are relative to New Zealand beaches.

Surrey: The south-east of England is the historical home of cricket and the first game ever was reputedly played in Surrey. It is a very green county with much woodland and many wealthy villages – home to wealthy commuters who work in London. Box Hill is near the centre of the county, has wonderful views and formed part of the course for the cycling road races at the 2012 Olympics.

Berkshire: Often referred to as The Royal County of Berkshire because it is where you will find Windsor Castle. The famed Eton College is in the area and was founded in 1440. Slough is the second city after Reading and was the fictional home to Ricky Gervais' comedy *The Office*.

Kent: With many orchards throughout the area, Kent is often known as the Garden of England. Canterbury and its cathedral was the inspiration for Chaucer's Canterbury Tales. The ferry to France leaves from Dover and looking back you see the White Cliffs. The Battle of Britain Museum is just outside Folkestone and is dedicated to this famous World War Two air-battle.

Essex: The reputation of Essex precedes it. Stereotypically, Essex girls are loud, brash, fun loving and dressed mainly in fake tan. Colchester claims to be the oldest town in Britain and was the capital of Roman Britain. The pier at Southend is the longest pleasure pier in the world.

Oxfordshire: Oxford is a beautiful city to visit and intellectually inspiring as you walk around. Blenheim Palace is a World Heritage site and the birth-place of Winston Churchill. The Chiltern Hills is an area of outstanding natural beauty. Go to Banbury to see the cross and you might even see a fine lady upon a white horse.

Buckinghamshire, Bedfordshire and Hertfordshire: These three counties are home to many commuters who work in London. Stoke Mandeville Hospital held a series of games for its disabled patients and this became the inspiration for The Paralympics. One of the 2012 Olympic mascots was named Mandeville in memory. Wycombe is so famous for furniture production that even its football team is nicknamed The Chairboys.

Bletchley Park has an amazing war history for decrypting code and today it is the site of the National Museum of Computing.

Norfolk & Suffolk: The derby between Ipswich (in Suffolk) and Norwich (in

Norfolk) is known as the Old Farm Derby, which demonstrates the importance of agriculture in these two counties. Sandringham House in Norfolk is owned by the royal family and the Queen holidays here. Newmarket is the home of British Horse racing and the National Horseracing Museum is located here. The Stour Valley in Suffolk is known as 'Constable Country' as this was where he painted so many of his landscapes.

Cambridgeshire: Cambridge is a beautiful city, lying on the banks of the River Cam. Parker's Piece (a park in the city) has its place in football history as it was after a kick-about that a group of students got together and drew up the first rulebook. These were referred to as the Cambridge Rules and they formed the basis for the official rulebook, which was created in London in 1863.

It is Cambridge University that makes the city and many famous New Zealanders have studied at Cambridge University. Among those alumni include Sir Francis Bell, the first New Zealand born Prime Minister, Wimbledon champion Anthony Wilding, Lord Ernest Rutherford, the Surgeon Harold Gillies, chemistry Nobel Prize winner Alan MacDiarmid and Baron Robin Cooke. Dame Kiri Te Kanawa is an honorary fellow of Wolfson College.

Ascot Racecourse

Ascot, Berkshire, SL5 7JX
www.ascot.co.uk

The highlight of the racing year at Ascot is undoubtedly Royal Ascot – the five-day festival in mid-June, which the Queen attends every day and the racing is of the highest standard.

The meeting dates back to the early 1700s when it was founded by Queen Anne. Each day the meeting commences once the royal entourage have arrived in a procession of horse-drawn carriages. Ascot is located only six miles from Windsor Castle, where The Queen is in residence for the week.

There is at least one group race held each day of the Royal meeting. Some of the racing highlights include the Gold Cup, the Coronation Stakes and the Golden Jubilee Stakes.

In memory of the meeting's founder, The Queen Anne Stakes is the first race on the opening day of the meeting. In 2011 champion New Zealand bred, formerly Australian trained and raced, So You Think, competed in the Prince of Wales Stakes on the second day of the meeting. He was a heavily backed favourite, but lost by a neck to Rewilding. In 2012 he returned and won the same race.

In 2008 the first New Zealand horse to run at Royal Ascot was the very successful Seachange. She came to England having won seven Group one races in New Zealand including the 1,000 Guineas in 2005 and the Telegraph Handicap in 2007. She contested the Golden Jubilee Stakes in 2008 but struggled throughout and finished well down the field.

New Zealand citizens can apply for badges for the Royal Enclosure for the Royal meeting. Tickets are expensive, are often over-subscribed and you must dress in formal wear – including a top hat for men – but from all accounts it is one of the best days you can have in racing.

Each year, 300,000 people go to the meeting making it the most attended meeting in Europe.

Race meetings take place outside of the Royal meeting, and the most prominent events are the King George VI and Queen Elizabeth Stakes which is run in July, and British Champions Day in October. While race meetings outside of Royal Ascot do not reach the same levels of formality, it is still a wonderful occasion to dress up and go to Ascot.

Going to Ascot is a great chance to appreciate the beauty of the surroundings and to think about the history of the horses and punters who have won and lost over the years. Three centuries of ripped up betting slips, 'sure thing', winners and 'if onlys'. You may even make a quid or two on the day, and that's not a bad thing!

Beach House Park Bowling Green, Worthing

Beach House Park, Lyndhurst Road, Worthing, West Sussex, BN11 2EJ
www.worthing.gov.uk and www.worthingbirdman.co.uk

Situated on the south coast, the Beach House Park Bowling Greens are the headquarters of Bowls England and have twice hosted the Men's World Championships in 1972 and 1992 as well as the Women's World Championships in 1977.

There are few grandmothers who win World Championships but New Zealand's Elsie Wilkie was 55 when she retained her World Championship Singles title on the Beach House Park greens in 1977.

Wilkie had won the World title four years earlier in Wellington and she retained her title at Beach House Park with 10 victories in the round-robin style competition. She had to win both her games on the last day against Papua New Guinea and then Welsh opponents. She won both matches comfortably and the title was hers.

For her two world championships, along with eight national titles, Wilkie is a member of the New Zealand Sports Hall of Fame.

Also in the Hall of Fame is fellow bowler Cis Winstanley. Aged almost 70 in 1977, she skippered the New Zealand triples team to silver at Beach House Park. Winstanley recalled years later about Worthing that 'New Zealand greens are eight feet shorter than theirs so we really had to heave those bowls'.

Did you know: The town of Worthing is also famous for its annual Birdman competition, which takes place in mid-summer from the town's pier. It is a flight competition for human-powered flying machines. The competition originally started along the coast in Selsey and then moved to Bognor Regis before its current home at Worthing. Ridiculous costumes, madcap machines and English eccentricity, all in the name of charity, make for a fun day out.

Bisley Shooting Range

Bisley Camp, Brookwood, Woking, GU24 0NY
www.bisleyshooting.co.uk

This shooting range in Surrey was home to the Shooting events for the 1908 and 1948 Olympic Games and the 2002 Commonwealth Games.

While the Games in 2002 were based in Manchester, the shooting took place here because there was not a more suitable local location.

In the 1948 Olympics the star at Bisley was the Hungarian shooter Karoly Takacs. In 1938 as a Sergeant in the army and a fine marksman, a grenade destroyed Takac's right hand. While recovering, he taught himself to shoot with his left hand. At the Olympics 10 years after his accident, he won the gold medal, broke the world record and then retained his title four years later at Helsinki.

New Zealand's Nadine Stanton did not need to overcome such adversity but in 2002, she also won a gold medal. She teamed up with Teresa Borrell to win Women's Double Trap Pairs in the Commonwealth Games and in the individual competition she won a silver medal.

Four New Zealand women won bronze medals in 2002. Diane Collings (Open Fullbore) and Juliet Ethrington (50 metre Prone Rifle) both finished third in their events as did Jocelyn Lees (25 metre Pistol) and Lees then teamed up with Tania Corrigan to claim bronze in the 25 metre pairs event.

Bisley was originally scheduled to host the 2012 Olympic shooting events but this was changed after the IOC were concerned that too many events were taking place outside London. This decision frustrated the national federations who thought spending large amounts of money on a temporary venue was an inefficient use of money.

In 2012 the Olympic shooting events took place at a temporary shooting range at the Royal Artillery Barracks at Woolwich, south-east London.

Brands Hatch

Fawkham, Longfield, Kent, DA3 8NG
www.brandshatch.co.uk

This racing circuit in Kent alternately hosted (along with Silverstone) the British Formula One Grand Prix from 1964 through until 1986.

No New Zealander has won the British Grand Prix but Denny Hulme was second in 1966. Two years later Hulme's countryman Chris Amon also finished runner-up after a 30-lap battle. Amon finished behind Jo Siffert who tragically died on the Brands Hatch track in 1971 after his car crashed and then caught fire.

In 1966 at Brands Hatch, McLaren Racing scored their first ever point at the circuit when Bruce McLaren drove the car to sixth place and one point. This was the first of many successes for the team and all New Zealanders should be incredibly proud of their achievements. Up to the end of the 2011 season the team has claimed eight manufacturers' titles and 12 drivers' titles.

In 1970, Denny Hulme returned to racing at Brands Hatch after the tragic death of Bruce McLaren. Hulme had missed the races in Belgium and the Netherlands to mourn his friend, teammate and countryman. Hulme raced valiantly and finished third in McLaren's honour.

Two years later, in 1972, New Zealand's Chris Amon finished in fourth, just one place ahead of Hulme. Amon is rated by some critics as one of the best drivers of all time, but he is also considered to be Formula One's unluckiest driver. In 13 years he raced in over 100 Grand Prix and led for more than 180 laps but he never won a race. Famed racing driver Mario Andretti once said of Amon's luck: 'if he became an undertaker, people would stop dying'.

The final Formula One race at Brands Hatch was in 1986, from which point Silverstone became the permanent home of the British Grand Prix.

Brands Hatch also hosted the first ever A1 Grand Prix race. In that race New Zealand's Matt Halliday finished third in the sprint race and fourth in the main race.

In motorcycling, Hugh Anderson won the 1966 Mellano Trophy and in 1999, Barry and Jane Fleury finished in the top 10 in the round of the Sidecar World Cup. In 2012, the track hosted the cycling road races for the Paralympics.

Carrow Road, Norwich

Carrow Road, Norwich, NR1 1JE
www.canaries.co.uk

This is the home of English football side, Norwich City.

It is with this club that New Zealand's most famous footballer, Wynton Rufer, was offered his first professional contract.

Sadly for Norwich fans, Rufer never played more than a friendly game for the Canaries, as he was unable to secure a work permit.

Rufer then signed for FC Zurich and consequently played in Switzerland and Germany throughout the 1980s and 90s. Rufer scored the winning goal for Werder Bremen in the 1992 European Cup Winners' Cup final in Lisbon versus Monaco.

Wynton's younger brother Shayne was also offered a contract at the same time but was likewise denied a work permit.

Norwich became the first football club to secure back-to-back promotions to reach the Premier League since Manchester City did the same thing in 2000.

Known as the Canaries, the club play in a yellow and green strip. Their rivalry with Ipswich is intense and eagerly anticipated on the calendar.

Chelsea College of Education, Eastbourne

Netball courts no longer exist
Address: Hillbrow, Denton Road, Eastbourne, BN20 7SR

The first ever Netball World Championships were held on the courts of this college in Eastbourne on England's south coast in the summer of 1963.

The International Federation had only been formed three years earlier after representatives from New Zealand, Australia, England, South Africa and the West Indies had met in Sri Lanka to discuss a standard set of rules.

One of their first agreements was a World Championship held every four years.

Held over 13 days in August 1963, 11 teams played each other in a round robin of matches. The title-deciding match was between New Zealand and Australia, which Australia edged by a single point 37-36. At the time it was called the World Tournament.

New Zealand won all of their other matches to finish second – ahead of the hosts England.

Cowes – Isle of Wight

Aberdeen Asset Management Cowes Week, Cowes,
Isle of Wight, PO31 7QN
www.cowes.co.uk and www.aamcowesweek.co.uk

The stretch of water between the south coast of England and the Isle of Wight is the Solent and its double tides make it an exciting place for offshore yacht racing.

Emirates Team New Zealand competing as part of Aberdeen Asset Management Cowes Week 2011.

Aberdeen Asset Management Cowes Week

Annually at the start of August, the Isle of Wight is home to the world-famous Cowes Week festival regatta – now known as Aberdeen Asset Management Cowes Week – a key component of the British social calendar alongside events such as Royal Ascot, Henley rowing regatta and Wimbledon. But Cowes Week regatta is much more than girls in pretty skirts, posh blokes and a big party – it is one of the world's great annual sailing festivals.

It has been held every year since 1826, except during the two World Wars. Over the week, more than a thousand boats compete in over 40 races. In 2011 the festival attracted more than 100,000 visitors to the island.

Over the years there has been an increase in racing close to shore, which makes the events even more exciting for spectators.

One of the famous trophies awarded during Cowes Week is the Queen's Cup – first raced for in 1897. Many New Zealanders have sailed at Cowes during the Week – both professionally as well as for fun.

The Admiral's Cup originally started life as a race between the USA and the UK as part of Cowes Week but was soon moved to a festival in its own right and entry was opened to all countries.

It was around the island of Cowes, that the America's Cup first came to prominence. *The America* won the Squadron Cup on 22 August 1851 in a time of just under 11 hours. The competition has been known as the America's Cup ever since.

The America's Cup

To celebrate the 150th anniversary of the America's Cup, a race around the Island was staged on 22 August 2001. Seventeen boats that had won or competed in the America's Cup raced at Cowes in a spectacular display of historic boats on the water.

The Cup itself was on display at a time when New Zealand were the holders. Commodore Peter Taylor of the Royal New Zealand Yacht Squadron rather cruelly joked at the time: 'This is the only way the cup will get back to Cowes.'

The Admiral's Cup

Held every two years, and organised by the Royal Ocean Racing Club, it took place off Cowes between 1957 and 1999. The winner was determined by the combined scores of three boats and included the Fastnet race.

New Zealand first raced for the Cup in 1971 with *Improbable* but 1971 is better remembered for Edward Heath skippering one of the winning British boats. Impressive … but more so when you know he was British Prime Minister at the time. Today, that seems not just improbable, more like impossible!

In 1975 New Zealand sent a full team of three boats for the first time and the team finished fifth. In 1981 the team again finished fifth but New Zealand's *Swuzzlebubble* was the leading boat.

After a sixth place finish in 1983, New Zealand made a concerted effort to win in 1987. Two years of planning, lots of practice, experience from the KZ7 America's Cup campaign, crewed by some of the world's best sailors and coached by Rod Davies, the team was unstoppable. *Propaganda* was skippered by Brad Butterworth and was the leading boat of the festival. All three New Zealand boats finished in the top six and New Zealand won with ease.

Dorney Lake

Eton College Rowing Centre, Dorney Lake,
Off Court Lane, Dorney, Windsor, SL4 6QP
www.dorneylake.co.uk

Dorney Lake is a rowing and canoeing centre near Windsor. It is owned by Eton College and hosted the rowing and canoeing events at the 2012 London Olympics.

It's debut on to the world stage came when it hosted the rowing World Cup in 2005 and then subsequently the World Championships in 2006. The highlight of these games of New Zealanders was when Mahe Drysdale pipped Germany's Marcel Hacker to the gold medal in the Single Scull and retained his title from the 2005 World Championships in Japan.

Drysdale was honoured as New Zealand's sportperson of the year – primarily for his World Championship victory.

In the same Championships, Nathan Twaddle and George Bridgewater as well as Juliette Haigh and Nicky Coles won silver medals in the men's and women's Coxless pairs. The Men's Coxed four won bronze as did Georgina and Caroline Evers-Swindell who could not repeat their Double Sculls title from Japan a year earlier.

At the 2012 Olympics, the lake was a gold mine for New Zealand. Four of New Zealand's six gold medals at the Olympics were won here.

Hamish Bond and Eric Murray won a gold medal in the Men's Pairs. They dominated the event from the start of the regatta to its conclusion. They won their heat by almost 10 seconds in world record time and cruised through their semi-final. The New Zealand pair won the final by more than five seconds and continued their unbeaten run in all competitions since teaming up in 2009.

Nathan Cohen and Joseph Sullivan were victorious in the Double Sculls beating the Italian pair in the final by more than a second.

Mahe Drysdale continued his imperious form at Dorney Lake in the Single Sculls by winning the gold medal from Ondrej Synek.

In the Women's Pair Juliette Haigh and Rebecca Scown claimed New Zealand's first Olympic medal on the lake with a bronze medal while Peter Taylor and Storm Uru also won bronze in the Men's Lightweight Double Sculls.

As well as rowing, the canoeing events took place on the lake and New Zealand's World Champion Lisa Carrington claimed the gold medal in the K1 200 Metres.

Fratton Park

Frogmore Road, Portsmouth, PO4 8RA
www.portsmouthfc.co.uk

This is the home of Portsmouth Football Club.

It was here that New Zealand's Chris Wood made his debut for West Bromwich Albion as a 17-year-old and became only the fifth New Zealander to play in the Premiership.

There are certain English football stadiums that appear desolate when not in use, seem to hark to a bygone era, seem too small, but come alive on match days when 21,000 fans are screaming. The proximity of the stands to the pitch at Fratton Park means the noise is magnified and suddenly everything becomes intense and electric. Even the best teams dread going to the Fratton Park cauldron.

Brian Turner played for the All Whites during their successful run to the 1982 World Cup and had previously played for Portsmouth during the 1969-70 season.

The All Blacks also played one game at Fratton Park in 1924. On the Invincibles tour, the All Blacks beat Hampshire 22 – 0, their 25th consecutive win on tour.

Goodwood Racing Circuit

Goodwood Estate, Chichester, West Sussex, PO18 0PH
www.goodwood.com

Primarily, the locations in this book are about happy times for New Zealanders, places where sports stars have plied their trade and succeeded – often against huge odds. But the Goodwood circuit is one of the few places tinged with sadness as it was here in on Lavant Straight that Bruce McLaren tragically died when on 2 June 1970 his car crashed into an unmanned flag station.

He was testing the Can-Am M8D for the upcoming series – of which he was the reigning champion.

Bruce McLaren had made his name racing in New Zealand and was the first driver to be offered the Driver in Europe scholarship. He wowed the racing world in Formula Two and was offered a seat in the Cooper Formula One team. At age 22, he became the youngest ever winner of a Formula One race – a record only broken by Fernando Alonso 44 years later. He finished third in the 1960 Championship.

He set up McLaren Racing in 1963 and the team is going at full speed today. In 1967 fellow New Zealander Denny Hulme won the F1 drivers title for the team.

Bruce McLaren was not only a great racing driver – he was also a great engineer and race car designer. He led the team with vision and it succeeded through innovation, teamwork and a good old-fashioned Kiwi ethos of hard work.

There is a memorial at the Goodwood circuit to Bruce McLaren. The epitath reads: 'Engineer, Constructor, Champion and Friend.'

In 1992 Denny Hulme drove an M8D at Goodwood to honour his former teammate and friend. Hulme then teamed up with enthusiastic New Zealand motor sport supporter Dr Shigeru Miyano to compete in a fuel economy challenge around Britain's coastal route drive. A year later Bruce McLaren's daughter Amanda competed with Dr Miyano in the same race.

Every year Goodwood hosts the Festival of Speed in mid-summer and it is considered to be the largest motoring party in the world with hundreds of thousands of people marvelling at all manner of cars, motorbikes and motorsport superstars.

The Goodwood Revival is held in September. The Revival offers visitors of all ages a chance to revel in the romance and glamour of motor racing as it used to be. It is the only sporting event in the world set entirely to a period theme and, every year, spectators and competitors take a magical step back in time by getting into the effervescent Goodwood spirit.

The majority of visitors enter into the spirit of the event, dressing in appropriate clothing from the 1940s, 50s and 60s. The event offers a weekend of historic motor racing, period theatre for all the family and scintillating on-track action.

Lakeside Country Club

Frimley Green, Camberley, Surrey, GU16 6PT
www.lakesidecomplex.com

Since 1986, the British Darts Organisation (BDO) World Championship has been held at this 1,400-seat venue in Surrey, 30 miles south-west of London.

The BDO acronym is important as there are two rival Darts organisations and two rival World Championship events. The BDO World Championship held at the Lakeside in early January has a longer history and a series of closer fought finals.

While crowds at the PDC (Professional Darts Corporation) event are generally more boisterous, supporters of the BDO event believe there is a greater focus on darts as sport rather than darts as entertainment. In 2007 BDO spokesman Robert Holmes said about their rival: 'It's just one big booze up and the darts is secondary.'

There is definitely no love lost between the two rival organisations.

At the Lakeside, Raymond van Barneveld won the World Championship four times before he controversially joined the rival PDC in 2006. Martin 'Wolfie' Adams has won the title three times, including back to back titles in 2010 and 2011.

Only one New Zealander has competed at the Lakeside. In 1993 the last World Darts Championship prior to the split, Peter Hunt lost in the first round to Scotland's Ronnie Sharp. In 1995 Hunt became the first Kiwi to win a first round World Championship match when he beat Stefan Eeckelaert from Belgium 3-0. In the second round, Hunt lost to England's Colin Monk in a tight match.

Hunt did not appear again at the Lakeside until 2003 and then made his final appearance a year later and on both occasions he lost in the first round.

While the name Lakeside is immediately connected to darts, through the year it is a popular cabaret club with on site hotels, lodges, separate ballroom and disco.

Madejski Stadium, Reading, Berkshire

Royal Way, Reading, RG2 0FL
www.readingfc.co.uk

The first game played on this ground was in 1998 and the stadium is named after businessman John Madejski.

The stadium was originally built as a football stadium for Reading but has become multi-purpose over the years as it became home to Premiership rugby side London Irish.

The Kiwis played on the ground at the 2000 Rugby League World Cup and beat Cook Islands by 84-10. On the day, 11 different players scored tries for the Kiwis.

A crowd of fewer than 4,000 turned up to watch that match, but Reading regularly saw full houses during their years in the Premier League between 2006 and 2008. They returned to the Premiership for the start of the 2012 season.

Before moving to the new stadium, Reading had played at Elm Park for over 100 years. But the club had greater ambitions and it was deemed uneconomic to redevelop the ground. After Reading moved, the stadium was demolished and the site became a housing estate.

London Irish play in England's premier rugby division. The team is nicknamed the Exiles, as the side was originally formed by Irishmen living in London but today it is sprinkled with players from across the world.

New Zealander Jarrod Cunningham was playing with London Irish in 2002, when he was diagnosed with Lou Gehrig's disease. He immediately retired from rugby and set up a foundation to educate and raise awareness about the disease. He was awarded the IRB Spirit of Rugby award in 2004 and died at home in New Zealand in 2007.

McLaren's F1 Base

Chertsey Road, Woking, Surrey, GU21 4YH
www.mclaren.com

The McLaren site at Woking, Surrey, is one of the leading automotive factories in the world. Modern, cutting edge technology is driving forward the next generation of Formula One Cars and that innovation is fed through to their road cars.

The McLaren team has undeniable Kiwi roots and it is a company New Zealand is right to be proud of. The team was formed when Project 4 merged with the McLaren team in 1980 – 10 years after the passing of founder New Zealand's Bruce McLaren.

Pre and post-merger, the team has won 12 drivers' championships and eight constructors' championships.

The team's founder is still remembered. To celebrate the 40th anniversary of his death, a minute's noise was held at the Woking factory. At the time McLaren team principal, Martin Whitmarsh described Bruce as having: 'the inspiration, vision and determination to take on and beat the greatest teams in motorsport…Bruce's values have seen us maintain a winning legacy throughout six decades of competition.'

The original logo for the McLaren team was designed by artist Michael Turner and featured a Kiwi. While unconfirmed, many believe the current logo is still a stylised version of a Kiwi.

Portman Road, Ipswich

Portman Road, Ipswich, IP1 2DA
www.itfc.co.uk

Portman Road has been the home stadium of Ipswich Town Football Club for over 125 years. The team is known as the Tractor Boys because of the area's rich agricultural history.

While the team was founded in 1878, they did not turn professional until

1936 and joined the Football League two years later. Their most fiercely contested match of the year is versus Norwich City – better known as the East Anglian derby.

Ipswich won the League title in 1961-62 and the FA Cup in 1978. They are also one of only seven English teams to have won on the European stage, when they won the UEFA Cup in 1981.

Three New Zealanders have recently played for Ipswich Town. Lee Norfolk became the first New Zealander to play in the Premiership when he played his only game for Ipswich in February 1995 against Southampton at Portman Road.

More recently, English born Tommy Smith has played for Ipswich, since graduating from the Ipswich youth academy. His form for the Tractor Boys led to a call up to the All Whites, a place at the 2010 World Cup finals where he played every minute of all three matches.

Rory Fallon also played at Portman Road on a short-term loan spell during 2010-11 making six appearances and scoring a solitary goal against Coventry.

The All Blacks also played at Portman Road when they beat a South-Eastern Counties team on 1 March 1954 by 21-13. A try scorer that day was a loose forward called Bill McCaw – a distant relative of the future All Blacks captain.

This was the only ever match the All Blacks played in March in the UK. While this was the last match of the UK leg tour, which had started in October, the team also played five matches in USA and Canada on the journey home.

Roger Bannister Running Track

Jackdaw Lane, Iffley Road, Oxford, OX4 1EQ
www.sport.ox.ac.uk

Oxford University is famed for the calibre of graduates it produces – the smartest, the brightest and the best.

No matter the field, from chemistry to economics, from politicians to Nobel Prize winners – the great and the good have graced the University.

Its running track is also the site of one sport's most famous moments. It was here, on 6 May 1954, that Roger Bannister broke the mythical barrier of the four-minute mile, in a track meeting when he was competing against the

University. One of his two pacemakers on the day was Chris Brasher, who in future years helped to found the London Marathon.

Interestingly six years earlier, Bannister as an undergraduate, was president of the University's athletic club and had set about replacing the bumpy track with a new one, which opened in 1950.

When the track was again refurbished in 2007 the track was renamed in his honour. Inside the Sports Complex is a small cabinet, which holds artefacts relating to the day in May 1954, one of the stopwatches, the lap bell, finishing post and some of the original track cinder. Visitors are more than welcome to pop in and view the display and walk the track as long as no events are taking place.

From a New Zealand perspective, Jack Lovelock was an Oxford blue and raced on the track while at University. He set the world record in 1932 for 1,320 yards of 3 minutes 2.4 seconds and a British all-comers record of 4 minutes 12 seconds.

Both Jack Lovelock and Roger Bannister were at Exeter College, Oxford. Not surprising when you consider that the Exeter College held the world's first official athletics meeting in 1850.

New Zealand's Amateur Athletic Association was formed in 1887, and alongside the Czech Association, both are recognised by the IAAF as the two oldest national bodies in the sport.

It has been argued that New Zealand's strength in athletics relative to its population is because athletics does not have a long history or tradition and so New Zealand was better able to become a pioneer in the sport.

New Zealand's only ever Olympic medal winning sprinter also attended Oxford University and set a 100-yard record on the track. Arthur Porritt ran 9.9 seconds while studying medicine.

As part of the sporting complex that is Iffley Road, the All Blacks have played six times at the neighbouring stadium. In 1905, Jimmy Hunter scored five of the 13 tries and ran out 47-0 winners. The Daily Express described the match as: 'The eyes feasted while the heart hungered.' The All Blacks beat the University again in 1924, 1935, 1953 and 1963.

As was often the case for the tours in the 1970s, the All Blacks were playing regional sides rather than local sides and in 1972, they beat Southern Counties 23-6 in their last game at Iffley Road.

Royal St George's Golf Club

Sandwich, Kent, CT13 9PB
www.royalstgeorges.com

In 2011 Royal St George's (Sandwich) hosted golf's British Open for the 14th time. It was the first course outside of Scotland to stage the Open back in 1894.

It is also the course where the first New Zealander competed. In 1949 Alex Murray, a professional from Titirangi West Auckland, missed the cut with rounds of 79 and 75. South Africa's Bobby Locke won from Ireland's Harry Bradshaw.

Up to and including 2012, 18 New Zealanders have competed at the British Open.

No New Zealander has threatened when Royal St George's has been the host. Simon Owen has been the best to date – finishing 23rd in 1981. In 2003 David Smail and Craig Perks both missed the cut while Michael Campbell finished 13 shots behind Open debutant Ben Curtis.

Curtis was the first debutant to win a Major since Francis Ouimet won the US Open in 1913. To write that Curtis' victory was unlikely at the start of the week is an understatement: 500 – 1 with the bookies, his first time in a major and he had never played on a links golf course.

This was his first trip to the UK – so much so that he and his wife came over a couple of days before the tournament so they could go sightseeing around London. It is the most unlikely, yet romantic, of Open victories.

Southampton Harbour

Southampton Harbour, Town Quay, Southampton, SO14 2AQ
www.southamptonvts.co.uk

Southampton Harbour has been the backdrop to some of the iconic images of New Zealand sport.

In 1990 Peter Blake was aboard *Steinlager 2* as it sailed into the harbour to claim the clean sweep of all six legs in the Whitbread Round the World Race. *Fisher & Paykel* skippered by Grant Dalton, finished second.

Southampton was the starting and final port for the 1989-90, 1993-94 and 1997-98 races and it was also the starting point for the 2001-02 race.

In 1994 Grant Dalton skippered *NZ Endeavour* to victory. New Zealand's Chris Dickson claimed the final leg honours for *Tokio* but he finished the overall race in eighth position.

It was a stellar sailing year for New Zealand as Ross Field led *Yamaha* to win the W60 class.

From Southampton Harbour you can take the ferry directly to the Isle of Wight. Go to Cowes during August and see the famous Cowes Week festival.

Many cruise ships depart from the harbour and you can often see some of the world's largest ships in port.

Warblington Graveyard, Warblington

Church of St Thomas à Becket, Church Lane, Warblington, PO9 2TU
www.warblingtonchurch.org.uk

In December 2001 New Zealand lost a sporting hero when Sir Peter Blake was shot dead by pirates on the Amazon river.

New Zealand's then Prime Minister Helen Clark travelled to England for Blake's funeral at Church of St Thomas à Becket, Warblington, and spoke at the service, describing the sailor as a 'living legend'.

The church is near Emsworth, Hampshire, where Blake and his family lived.

Blake's headstone includes words from the poem, Sea-Fever by John

Masefield: 'I must down to the sea again, to the lonely sea and sky, and all I ask is a tall ship and a star to steer her by...'

New Zealanders are known to regularly visit the adjacent graveyard to pay their respects and to write messages in the church's visitors' book. As a sign of respect, New Zealanders have traditionally left New Zealand coins or red socks at the grave.

Wentworth Golf Club, Surrey

Wentworth Drive, Virginia Water, Surrey, GU25 4LS
www.wentworthclub.com

The Wentworth Club was built in the 1920s as a retreat for busy people to escape the hustle and bustle of London. Today, it is still a peaceful haven set in the Surrey countryside – popular with the wealthy and glamorous set.

The West Golf Course is the jewel in the Wentworth crown. It was designed by renowned golf architect Harry Colt in 1926 and up until 2007, the course was home to the World Matchplay Championship.

The club is the headquarters to the European Tour and the West Course hosts the premier European event on the golfing calendar – the British PGA, which is held at the end of May. As well as the West Course, the resort is home to the East course and the newly built Edinburgh course.

The green fees are not cheap – in Summer 2011 the West Course was £360 but this does include your own personal caddy.

New Zealand sports fans will be walking in the footsteps of golfing history. In 1969, Bob Charles beat Gene Littler in the final of the World Matchplay Championships on the last hole. Charles had lost to Gary Player the year before.

Charles had previously won the 1962 Daks tournament on the course – a title he shared with Welshman Dai Rees.

Between the inaugural World Matchplay Championship in 1964 and 1971, the title was shared between the big three of Arnold Palmer, Gary Player and Jack Nicklaus – except in 1969 when Charles was victorious.

The tournament had been devised by the late Mark McCormack – the founder of super sports agency IMG. Arnold Palmer was the company's first client and IMG took the game to a global audience. No contract between Palmer and IMG was ever signed as the deal was done on a handshake of trust.

After McCormack's death he was inducted into both the Golf and Tennis Halls of Fame – and today's multimillionaire golfers and tennis players can all say thank you to the work IMG did to promote their games.

Simon Owen was runner-up almost 10 years later in 1978 – losing in the final to Japan's Isao Aoki.

In 2005, on the back of his US Open triumph at Pinehurst, Michael Campbell beat Geoff Ogilvy, Steve Elkington and Retief Goosen en route to the World Matchplay final. Campbell claimed the title with a 2 and 1 victory over Ireland's Paul McGinley.

Local Wentworth resident Ernie Els won the title a record seven times including the last title Wentworth was the host to in 2007.

The West Course has also hosted the Ryder Cup in 1953 – when USA beat the UK by $6^{1/2}$ to $5^{1/2}$.

Windsor Great Park

The Savill Garden, Wick Lane, Englefield Green, Surrey, TW20 0UU
www.theroyallandscape.co.uk

This park south of Windsor is owned by the Crown Estates and was historically a royal hunting ground and deer still roam the park in honour of its origins.

In the 1948 London Olympics, the Park was the home to the Cycling road race. It was originally planned to take place in Richmond Park, but this was prohibited by law.

King George VI gave permission to stage the cycling race at the Great Park and a seven-mile lap was designed. The Duke of Edinburgh started the race and in torrential rain the cyclists took off in front of 15,000 spectators. Seventeen laps meant a race over 120 miles.

New Zealand's Nick Carter lined up at the start line but crashed in the terrible weather and did not finish the race. Like the other New Zealanders who competed that year, Carter had travelled to London by boat – taking 31 days. Carter did his best to keep fit – even using rollers to try and balance his bike onboard. It proved difficult and according to Carter: 'the sea was too choppy and I was forever falling off'.

The road race was eventually won by Jose Beyaert from France and Belgium took the team gold medal.

International polo is played in the park at Smith's Lawn and the grounds have hosted Coronation Cup matches between New Zealand and England.

The Test was the highlight of the Cartier International Polo Day, which has been running since the mid 1980s and is popular with royalty, rock stars and celebrities alike. England won 9-7 on the day and has won four out of the five times the two teams have played for the Coronation Cup. New Zealand's sole victory came in 1991.

For gardening fans, the largest New Zealand native garden in the UK is at Windsor Great Park. There are over 3,000 native New Zealand plants as part of the Savill Garden. It was designed by New Zealand landscape Gardener Sam Martin who has lived in the UK for over 10 years.

South West

Rolling green fields, a seemingly more relaxed and laid-back lifestyle, the coast is always close and agriculture and tourism are integral to the economy.

With such a description, this could be New Zealand, not the south-west of England.

The sporting fields of this area match many of New Zealand's experiences. Rugby competes with football in popularity. Horse racing and Equestrian are important, and New Zealanders have won World Championship shearing events at the Royal Show in Bath. Even the All Blacks gained their iconic name in this region.

A highlight of the South West is to spend a day lazing on a beach in Cornwall.

Somerset is traditional and more sparsely populated than other areas of Great Britain. Bath is a beautiful Roman city renowned for elegant architecture. The Devon coastline is spectacular to walk along while the tourist heartbeat pumps in Cornwall during the summer.

The spa town of Cheltenham is elegant and refined but when the visitors descend for the annual horse racing festival in March the town is transformed into a great big party.

Across the Cotswolds, you will find honey coloured homes – like the post-cards, only real.

Take a moment to remember New Zealand soldiers from World War One. On the hill near Bulford in Wiltshire is an image of a Kiwi carved by soldiers waiting to go home after the war finished.

Stare at Stonehenge and like millions before you and wonder 'Why, how, who …'

Visit the Clifton Suspension Bridge across the Avon Gorge in Bristol and admire the engineering greatness of its designer Isambard Kingdom Brunel.

Ashton Gate, Bristol

Ashton Road, Bristol, BS3 2EJ
www.bcfc.co.uk

This stadium is home to Bristol City Football Club and the All Blacks have twice played here.

Bristol City finished second in the top flight in 1906, and reached the FA Cup final in 1909, where they lost to Manchester United. They were relegated two years later and did not return to the top flight until 1976.

They remained in the top division for four years but then suffered three consecutive relegations, decimating the club, and leaving it bankrupt.

The club has since returned to the second division of the English game and is now looking to return to the top division. The club signed New Zealander Chris Wood in January 2012 for a six-month loan period and he scored a goal in his first game at Ashton Gate.

The All Blacks have twice played at the stadium. On the 1997 tour they beat an English Rugby Partnership XV 18-11. On that tour the All Blacks played warm up games at the grounds they would play World Cup matches on in 1999.

In the 1999 World Cup the All Blacks beat Tonga 45-9 to kick-start their campaign. This was Tonga's first ever match against the All Blacks. The All Blacks were sloppy but Jonah Lomu scored two tries.

Norm Maxwell also scored a try in this game – remarkably all five tries he scored in tests were against Pacific Island nations.

Bristol City have planning permission to build a new 30,000 seat stadium and move away from Ashton Gate, but this move is proving controversial with some locals.

Badminton

Badminton Horse Trials, Badminton, Gloucestershire, GL9 1DF
www.badminton-horse.co.uk

The Mitsubishi Motors Badminton Horse Trials is one of the Majors in the Three Day Eventing world.

Set in the grounds of Badminton House in the Gloucestershire countryside, the Horse trials take place over four days at the start of May.

The dressage at Badminton is competed over two days, on Friday and Saturday; the cross country is on Sunday and the final day's showjumping takes place on the first Monday in May, which is a public holiday.

Together with the Three Day event at Kentucky and the Burghley Horse Trials, Badminton makes up the Rolex Grand Slam.

Mark Todd has won four times at Badminton. His first victory came in 1980, on his debut, aboard Southern Comfort III.

In 1994 he won again on Horton Point and two years later, he claimed victory aboard Bertie Blunt.

In 2011 after eight years away from the sport and as part of his comeback for the London Olympics, he claimed a fairytale victory aboard NZB Land Vision.

He also finished second in 1984 and 1985 aboard Charisma – the horse he rode to Olympic gold in Los Angeles and in Seoul. He was also runner-up in 1998 and 1999.

Andrew Nicholson was Mark Todd's groom when Todd first competed in 1980. Nicholson now holds the record for competing at Badminton the most times – 30 times. His best finish is second in 2004 aboard Lord Killinghurst, when he finished behind Englishman William Fox-Pitt.

Badminton House is the country seat of the Duke of Beaufort and it has been in the family since the late 1600s.

The game of Badminton derives its name from the country home. A game with a shuttlecock was played indoors in the great hall of Badminton House. By 1877, the first rules were set out by the Bath Badminton Club and the game took off in popularity.

Cheltenham Race Course

Evesham Road, Prestbury, Cheltenham, GL50 4SH
www.cheltenham.co.uk

Set in the heart of the beautiful Cotswolds, nestled under Cleeve Hill, for race fans Cheltenham Racecourse is a little piece of heaven.

The course comes alive for four days in March when the Cheltenham Festival becomes the only show in town. The biggest four-day race meeting sees the city become the heart of the nation's sporting action and the biggest and best parties.

The festival often coincides with St Patrick's Day and is especially popular with Irish horse racing supporters. The bars are well stocked and when an Irish

Day 1 at the Cheltenham Festival.

horse comes in, the cheers can be heard across the county and beyond – by punters and pub landlords.

The course is the finest National Hunt Racecourse in the land and winning a Cheltenham Gold Cup can be the greatest moment for a jockey, trainer or owner.

The Gold Cup is just one of the many racing highlights of the Cheltenham Festival. Coming towards the end of the National Hunt racing season in March, the festival also includes such leading races as the Queen Mother Champion Chase, the World Hurdle and the Arkle Challenge Trophy.

But it is the Gold Cup on the final day, which captures most attention. Run over three miles two and a half furlongs (5.33kms) form horses tend to dominate and previous winners on the track often repeat their victories.

Golden Miller won it five times in the 1930s, Cottage Rake and Arkle both won three times, as did Best Mate between 2002 and 2004. Only Golden Miller in 1934 has ever gone on to win the Grand National at Aintree in April and he is honoured by a statue at the Cheltenham course.

There is also a statue on the course of Best Mate, which was sculpted by Philip Blacker. Before becoming a sculptor, Blacker was a jump jockey and was aboard New Zealand's best ever finisher in 1979, when Royal Mail finished second to Alverton. As a sad postscript, Alverton died trying to win the Grand National less than three weeks later.

County Cricket Ground, Bristol

The County Ground, Nevil Road, Bristol, BS7 9EJ
www.gloscricket.co.uk

This cricket ground is the home of Gloucestershire County Cricket Club and more New Zealand cricketers have played for Gloucestershire than any other county.

New Zealand played on the ground in the 1983 World Cup beating Sri Lanka but the team failed to qualify for the semi-finals. They also played one-day internationals against England on the ground in 2004 and 2008, winning both games.

W.G. Grace played his county cricket for Gloucestershire. The bearded all rounder who is viewed as one of the all time greats played first-class cricket for 44 seasons from 1865 through until 1908.

He played in Gloucestershire's first ever county match in 1870. The team was rated the Champion county four times prior to 1890, but since the start of the County Championship in that year, the best Gloucestershire has done is finishing runners-up six times.

Charles Dacre was the first New Zealander to play for Gloucestershire from 1928 through to 1936. From 1930 until 1935 he scored more than 1,000 runs each season for the County.

Dacre was a dual international having played four matches of football for New Zealand in 1922 and 1923. Dacre was also the first New Zealander to score a century at Lord's in 1927.

Other New Zealanders to have played for the county include Hamish Marshall, Sean Tracy, Justin Vaughan, Ian Butler, James Franklin, Kane Williamson and Craig Spearman. Aaron Redmond played T20 for the 2010 season and Geoff Howarth played for a season in 1969 for Gloucestershire Second XI.

Former New Zealand cricket coach John Bracewell held a similar role at Gloucestershire from 1998 to 2003 when he left and he returned to the club in 2009 as the director of cricket.

Bracewell was in the World Cup squad but did not play in the match against Sri Lanka. Sir Richard Hadlee was the man of the match as he took five wickets for 25. Sri Lanka was dismissed for 206 and New Zealand reached the target with more than 20 of the 60 overs to spare.

The ground is also known as Nevil Road. The ground in the past has been called: Ashley Down Ground, Fry's Ground, Phoenix County Ground and the Royal & Sun Alliance County Ground.

County Ground, Exeter

Stadium no longer exists
Approximate Address: Ferndale Road, Exeter, EX2 9BW

The All Blacks have been playing rugby in the UK since 16 September 1905. It was on that day the All Blacks played at the County Ground, Exeter, against Devon and kicked off the tour with a resounding victory.

There have been so many victories since that first game, but this one is special for two reasons. Firstly, it was the first ever New Zealand game on English soil. Secondly, the All Blacks name has a historical connection to this ground.

The All Blacks is the most recognisable brand in New Zealand – no matter where you go in the world, when they find out where you are from, the men in black is often one of the first topics of conversation.

On that September day New Zealand beat Devon by 55 – 4. It was a resounding thrashing. It was such a surprise that some newspaper editors assumed there must have been a mistake and so reversed the scoreline. But there was no mistake.

Based on the following nine games on tour, the only genuine surprise is that Devon scored. Against Cornwall, Bristol, Northampton, Leicester, Middlesex, Durham, Hartlepool Clubs, Northumberland, Gloucester and Somerset the tourists scored 353 points while only Durham managed three points. All other eight games were shutouts.

The All Blacks name has all of the attributes of a great brand – history, consistency, a culture of success, and it inspires passion among its supporters. It is a name that stirs all of our emotions – national pride, confidence and fear among opponents.

The myth of the All Blacks name is still debated today. Billy Wallace was on the tour committee and claims it came from erroneous reporting as they were meant to play like 'all backs'.

The conflicting view is that it was first used by Daily Mail writer J.A. Buttery who used the term after the Hartlepool game on 11 October.

Buttery followed the tour throughout and may have picked up a reference from the *Express & Echo* in Devon who used the term describing the first game: 'The All Blacks, as they are styled by reason of their sable and unrelieved costume, were under the guidance of their captain (Mr Gallaher), and their fine physique favourably impressed the spectators.'

It was also reported in Wellington's *Evening Post* that Ernie Booth, a fullback or three-quarter was partially responsible for the name. While training at West Ealing, Buttery was talking with Booth. They were looking at the tour's captain Dave Gallaher and George Gillett who were both wearing black belts and their elastic kneelets were dyed black. Buttery asked why and Booth explained jocularly: 'to be all black'. Buttery liked the phrase and then used it within his articles. Supporters as well as other English newspapers followed and by December, the trend had reached New Zealand as the Herald titled a regular column: All Black Gossip.

In Buttery's own book published after the tour, he makes no mention of the exchange with Booth. He wrote that it was because of the colour of the uniform. 'The only colour not black was the Silver Fern on the left breast and white of their boot laces.'

The All Blacks have played at the County Ground twice since that historic game in 1905. On the 1963-64 tour, they won 38 – 6 against South-Western Counties and in 1979, they beat South-West and South Division 16-0.

As well as rugby, the ground was bordered by a Speedway track used by the Exeter Falcons.

New Zealand's Ivan Mauger raced for the team between 1973 and 1977 and is renowned as the best to have ever ridden for the team. He won the World Speedway championship in 1974.

In October 2005 Ivan Mauger was given the honour of riding the last ever four laps around the track as a final farewell because the stadium was to be demolished to make way for a housing development. The housing development is named EX1905 in honour of the All Blacks famous victory.

County Ground, Taunton

Priory Ave, Taunton, Somerset, TA1 1JT
www.somersetcountycc.co.uk

This is the home of Somerset County Cricket Club – where they have been playing cricket since 1882.

Somerset has never won the County Championship, but in 2010 the team finished runners-up to Nottinghamshire.

A myth surrounds how New Zealander Tom Lowry came to play for Somerset.

In the 1920s, while at Cambridge University, he played 46 times for the County during summer vacations. The myth goes that he qualified to play for the County because he was born in Wellington. The authorities presumed that meant the small town seven miles south of Taunton, not New Zealand's capital – 11,000 miles further south. In reality, Lowry was born in Hawkes Bay, but over time it has become a story told over pints in the pubs of Somerset.

Lowry goes down in New Zealand cricketing history as he was the captain of New Zealand's first ever Test matches. As good as he was a player, he excelled in captaincy. He was once described as, 'a man more given to command than obey.' He was quick to spot the weaknesses in his opponents, he was innovative and he inspired confidence among his team.

The next New Zealander to play for Somerset was at the heart of controversy but none of his own doing. The Somerset side had been successful in the one-day game in the late 1970s and into the new decade but by the mid 1980s the team was ageing.

The new captain Peter Roebuck led the move to make changes, not renewing the contracts of West Indian stars Viv Richards and Joel Garner. New Zealand's Martin Crowe was brought in as the county's foreign star. Ian Botham was furious at the decision and quit in protest and moved to Queensland and then Worcestershire before joining Durham. The argument still seethes today.

The list of New Zealanders to play for the county is short. Other than Lowry and Crowe, Paul Unwin played one game for Somerset in 1989.

Andy Caddick was born in Christchurch, New Zealand and modelled his bowling to the style of Sir Richard Hadlee. While Caddick played age group cricket for New Zealand he played his entire professional career at Somerset and took 875 first class wickets. He played 62 Tests for England.

Foxhill Motocross Circuit

Foxhill Motocross Track, Callas Hill, Foxhills, Swindon, SN4 0DR
www.foxhillmx.com

This circuit in the Wiltshire countryside is held in high esteem by Motocross riders.

Created in the late 1980s, it was home to the Motocross British Grand Prix throughout the 1990s. In 1998 the circuit was under the spotlight as it held the Motocross des Nations – the first time it had been held in the UK since 1980.

This competition is a national team competition consisting of three Motocross races across three different classes – 125cc, 250cc and Open.

The New Zealand team was represented by Josh Coppins, Daryll King and Shayne King. This was the same team that represented New Zealand between 1995 and 2000.

The weather was awful, and the track quickly cut up, meaning the racers constantly had to battle with the mud. The weather was so bad that the second of the three races had to be stopped part-way through because the track had deteriorated so badly.

The New Zealand team finished on 49 points – in third place behind Belgium and Finland.

Home Park, Plymouth

Plymouth, PL2 3DQ
www.pafc.co.uk

Home Park is within Central Park in the northern suburbs of Plymouth.

Plymouth is the largest city in the UK not to have hosted top-flight football and the ground has been the team's home since in 1901.

Plymouth Argyle are known as the Pilgrims and the team play in green.

If you are watching football at Home Park, it is the furthest western and furthest southern Football League ground in England.

On 26 August 1978 Tony Levy made his first appearance for Plymouth off the bench in a 2-1 victory over Lincoln City. It was to be his only appearance. He left for Torquay at the end of the season and then moved to Yeovil. Eventually he moved to New Zealand and played six matches for the All Whites between 1988 and 1989.

New Zealander Rory Fallon signed with Plymouth Argyle in 2007 having previously been at Swansea, Swindon and Barnsley. He appeared more than 100 times for Plymouth and scored more than 20 goals for the team.

But it is his goal against Bahrain in Wellington that secured New Zealand's qualification to the World Cup that Fallon will be most remembered for.

Kingsholm Stadium, Gloucester

Kingsholm Road, Kingsholm, Gloucester, GL1 3AX
www.gloucesterrugby.co.uk

This rugby ground in Gloucester is one of only two grounds in England where New Zealand have played both Rugby World Cup matches and Rugby League World Cup matches.

The home of rugby in Gloucester saw the All Blacks beat USA in 1991 by 46-6 with John Wright scoring a hat-trick.

In the 2000 Rugby League World Cup, the Kiwis beat Lebanon by 64-0 in their first group match.

On that cold day at the end of October, as the commentators researched the Middle East nation, five New Zealanders scored a brace of tries against the team known as the Cedar Men.

This was the team's first step on the way to the final where they would eventually be beaten by Australia.

A host of New Zealanders have played rugby for Gloucester. Ian Jones, Carlos Spencer and Greg Somerville all played for the Red and Whites.

It was Gloucester who persuaded rugby league international Lesley Vainokolo to switch codes at the end of the 2007 season. The ground had happy memories for 'the Volcano' as he was one of the five New Zealanders who had scored twice against Lebanon seven years earlier. Vainokolo was hugely successful and within months, had already made his debut for the England rugby team against Wales in the Six Nations.

Royal Bath and West of England Society Showgrounds

The Showground, Shepton Mallet, Somerset, BA4 6QN
www.bathandwest.com

Home to the Royal Bath and West show, this annual agricultural show has hosted the World Shearing Championships three times.

In 1977 it was the first ever venue for the premier shearing event and it was again host in 1984 and most recently in 1992.

New Zealanders have dominated the event since its inception when in the inaugural event New Zealanders won the three major events. Roger Cox won the Singles and then teamed up with Godfrey Bowen to win the Teams' competition. Peter Casserly won the Blades event.

In 1984 John Fagan and Colin King teamed up to win the Teams' competition. That year Scotland born, but now New Zealand resident, Tom Wilson, won the Singles event beating John Fagan into second place.

In 1992 the last time Bath and South West hosted the event, the New Zealand domination continued as David Fagan won both the Shearing event and the team event with Kevin Walsh retaining the titles he had won in Masterton four years earlier. Tony Dobbs won the Blades event.

The show itself is an incredibly popular annual agricultural event, taking place at the end of spring. It attracts huge crowds and is considered to be the biggest event on the rural calendar and celebrates all aspects of farming and rural life in Britain today.

Weymouth Harbour

Osprey Quay, Portland, Dorset, DT5 1SA
www.wpnsa.org.uk

The sailing events at the 2012 London Olympics took part in this bay on the south coast.

Jo Alleh and Olivia Powrie won gold for New Zealand in the Women's 470 Class.

Also on the water, Peter Burling and Blair Tuke won silver in the Men's 470 Class.

Wales

It is a road sign as you drive along but it is always deeply gratifying when you leave England and cross into Wales. Whether it is the M4 Motorway in south Wales heading for Cardiff or Swansea or a country road in mid Wales it feels almost like a different world.

Wales is bilingual and every sign is in Welsh and English. It is impossible not to giggle, occasionally wondering how to pronounce everything.

For many New Zealanders, Cardiff will be the destination. In the past the All Blacks played at 'The Arms' but today it is at the magnificent Millennium Stadium. It is a majestic venue set near the city centre and there is a special buzz on match days.

Apart from the rugby, you can watch international cricket at the Swalec Stadium. The city hosted the Empire Games in 1958. The Cardiff art gallery exhibits works by Monet, van Gogh and a sculpture by Rodin.

But Wales is much more than Cardiff. Think more than dragons, choirs and daffodils. Keep going and head to Swansea, learn about the importance of coal to Wales and in particular the Swansea valleys.

Visit a Welsh village that is unpronounceable, go to the coast and look west – as far as the eye can see. Go to Cardigan Bay in mid Wales – after which the famous New Zealand racehorse was named.

Go to the Snowdon National Park and enjoy the outdoors. Here you can go walking or white water rafting, climbing or just chilling – this is a beautiful part of Wales.

Across the North Wales coast are a series of resort towns. Some such as Prestatyn and Rhyl are in need of love and attention. But in Llandudno you can hark back to a more simple time before low-cost airlines flew you abroad for holidays in the sun. Eat an ice cream, walk along the Victorian Pier and relax as life slows down.

The famed ring of castles across North Wales formed a strategic stronghold for King Edward in the 13th century. Conwy, Beaumaris and Caernarfon are amazing to visit from a historical perspective.

Is your surname Jones, Davies or Williams? Wales is even more wonderful to visit if you are a genealogist hunting your welsh ancestors. It is fascinating to think about what they left behind when they moved halfway across the world to New Zealand.

It is always a treat to visit Wales. Hwyl Fawr.

Aberdare Athletic Ground, Aberdare

Stadium no longer exists
Approximate Address: The Ynys, Aberdare, CF44 7RP

In South Wales, in the mining town of Aberdare, sporting history was made on New Year's Day 1908 as New Zealand played their first ever international rugby league match – the first between northern and southern hemisphere teams.

The choice of venue for rugby league's first ever Test match may appear strange at first, but it can be explained by the politics of sport, business and the rivalry between rugby league and union.

In 1907 Aberdare had lost its rugby team after it was expelled from the Welsh Rugby Union for paying a player. The Welsh rugby union investigated claims of professionalism at Aberdare and at local rivals Merthyr. Eight

Aberdare players were banned for life as were the entire committee but no one from Merthyr was punished. The town felt let down by the Rugby Union.

In the nearby valley, Merthyr was planning a rugby league team to join the northern league and when it was announced that Merthyr would be playing against the touring Kiwis in November, Aberdare's sporting pride was damaged further.

Rugby league's officials sensed an opportunity. As a working-class area with lower incomes, this seemed an ideal area for the new professional game and a big crowd at an international match could light a spark in popularity.

Originally, the Aberdare Athletic Association refused the application for rugby league to be played on their ground, but sensing the prospect of a large paying crowd, they eventually relented.

So on New Year's Day 1908 a crowd of 17,000 watched the All Golds take on Wales in a historic match for the sport. New Zealand's Arthur Kelly score rugby league's first ever international try and led 8-3 but the Kiwis were undone by a late try from Dai Jones and Wales claimed a 9-8 victory. Dick Wynard had the chance to win the match for New Zealand but dropped the ball right in front of the line.

Rugby league officials got their wish and a club was formed in Aberdare in March and played in the 1908-09 rugby league season. The Aberdare team lost its first game to Wigan 56-0, they won only one game all season and finished the season dead last. It was an 'ignominious failure'.

Clubs were expected to make profits, and after the club reported 'unexpected difficulties' at the end of that first season it resigned from the league and never played again.

The ground has long since been demolished and the site is now home to the Michael Sobell leisure centre.

So while Aberdare's own playing history was memorable only for failure, the town and the ground go down in the annals of rugby league history.

Cardiff Arms Park

Stadium no longer exists
Approximate Address: Westgate Street, Cardiff, CF10 1NS

The Arms was synonymous with Welsh rugby and the All Blacks played many matches against the Welsh prior to it being pulled down to make way for the highly impressive Millennium Stadium.

The stadium was also the home of the 1958 British Empire & Commonwealth Games.

But to most New Zealand sports fans, the Arms is a rugby venue, and it was one of the great venues to watch rugby. Matches between the Welsh and New Zealand were traditionally exciting contests with passionate crowds. Each team's supporters have always been respectful of the others' knowledge and desire to win.

Only in New Zealand and Wales is rugby the country's number one sport so matches between the two nations have always been ferocious – and occasionally controversial.

It was at Cardiff Arms Park, that rugby's most controversial moment happened. In 1905 the New Zealand team had won the first 30 games on tour including Tests against England and Scotland. They had outscored the opposition by 753 to 22.

Wales were the best team in the UK having recently won the Triple Crown, so New Zealand's first ever match at Cardiff Arms Park was dubbed 'The World Championship', pitting the two best teams head to head. The match also started with the crowd's rendition of Hen Wlad fy Nhadau (Land of Our Fathers) which is the first ever time an anthem was sung before a rugby test.

Wales took the lead with a try through Teddy Morgan.

Then, New Zealand's Billy Wallace broke free but was caught by Willie Llewellyn. He passed to Bob Deans who then headed for the try line. Rhys Gabe gave chase and so did the referee. To the day of his death, Deans claimed he had made the try line but was pulled back while Gabe was equally positive he was short. The referee blew 'no-try' and Wales were victorious.

Thirty years later, Wales beat New Zealand again at Cardiff Arms Park, 13-12.

It was third time lucky for the Welsh when the All Blacks returned on the 1953 tour. In the All Blacks 400th ever match Gareth Griffiths for Wales ignored medical advice and played through the pain of a dislocated shoulder and the men in scarlet won 13-8 with a late try by Ken Jones.

The Cardiff Arms Park omens had not been good leading up to that 1953 match. A month before the test, at Cardiff Arms Park, the All Blacks suffered a very rare event – a loss against a club or province. It has only ever happened eight times in the UK and in November 1953, Cardiff beat the All Blacks 8-3.

Wales have not beaten the All Blacks since that game in 1953.

The All Blacks did lose 23-11 at the Arms in 1973 to the Barbarians. That match will always be remembered for 'that try', in which Gareth Edwards scored the try of the century. The Barbarians ran it out from almost their own goal line. Cliff Morgan's commentary made the try even more memorable: 'This is Gareth Edwards, A dramatic start, what a score ... If the greatest writer of the written word would have written that story no one would have believed it.'

The All Blacks have, however, beaten Wales ever since 1953. On tours in 1963, 1967, 1972, 1978, 1980 and finally in 1989 were all victories to New Zealand at Cardiff Arms Park. It was close in 1978 (13-12 with a controversial late penalty kicked by Brian McKechnie after Andy Haden had duped the referee) but in 1989 New Zealand scored four tries and won 34-9.

After 1989 New Zealand would not play Wales again on Welsh soil until 2002, by which time the Millennium Stadium was being used.

As well as rugby, the stadium was home to the British Empire and Commonwealth Games in 1958 and New Zealand sent a team of 52 men and 12 women to compete.

Both the opening and closing ceremonies were held in the stadium. The Games were the first ever which featured the Queen's Baton Relay. Roger Bannister carried it out from Buckingham Palace's gates and Welsh rugby player and sprinter Ken Jones carried it into the stadium as part of the opening ceremony.

The closing ceremony was a proud moment for all Welsh people. The Queen was ill and could not attend the closing ceremony but in her message to the crowd, she officially appointed her son Charles, as the Prince of Wales.

At the time Cardiff Arms Park had terraces and room for 60,000 spectators but in preparation for the Games, seating was installed, so 34,000 people watched the athletic events.

They saw New Zealander Murray Halberg win the Men's three-mile race and Neville Scott finish third to take bronze. Halberg's margin of victory was about 60 yards and he won by almost 10 seconds. He took more than 20 seconds off the previous Games record and he had run the third fastest three-mile race ever.

Valerie Sloper won the Women's Shot Put. Sloper also won a bronze medal in the Discus behind her compatriot Jennifer Thomson. Mary Donaghy in the High Jump also won silver as did Les Mills in the Men's Discus.

Dave Norris (Men's Triple Jump) and Merv Richards (Men's Pole Vault) both won bronze medals.

In the first ever Women's Rugby World Cup held in 1991, NZ lost 7-0 in the semi-finals to the eventual winners USA at Cardiff Arms Park.

Llanelwedd, Builth Wells

Royal Welsh Showground, Llanelwedd, Builth Wells, Powys , LD2 3SY
www.rwas.co.uk

This is the site of the annual Royal Welsh Show and has twice hosted the World Championships for Sheep Shearing.

The Royal Welsh Show first hosted the World Championships in 1994 when the New Zealanders David Fagan and Alan McDonald won the Team event while McDonald won the Single event from Fagan.

David Fagan won a bigger prize in 1994. He met his future wife Wendy at the event who had gone to watch the show jumping.

Fagan was again runner-up in the Singles event in 2010 when the event returned to Llanelwedd – this time to Cam Ferguson. The two paired up to win the Team event.

In the wool handling, New Zealand's Sheree Alabaster and Keryn Herbert were victorious in the 2010 Team event.

In 2010 more than 230,000 people attended the Royal Welsh Show over the four days. As well as the world's best sheep shearers, they also saw the JCB Dancing Diggers, wood chopping, food halls, bands, stalls, vintage agricultural machines and a man who shepherded ducks!

Llyn Padarn

Gilfach Ddu, Llanberis, Caernarfon, LL55 4TY
www.lake-railway.co.uk

A glacially formed lake, (Llyn is Welsh for lake) at the foot of Mount Snowdon, was the home for the rowing competition as part of the 1958 British Empire and Commonwealth Games.

The majority of the Games were held in Cardiff, but this lake is 160 miles north of the Welsh capital.

The New Zealand team won a treble of medals on the lake.

Bob Parker and Reginald Douglas had won gold in the Men's Coxless Pairs at the Games four years earlier in Vancouver and they returned to defend their title. They succeeded, beating the English pair by three seconds.

On Llyn Padarn, James Hill won two medals. He won a silver medal in the Single Sculls and teamed up with Norman Suckling to win a bronze in the Double Sculls.

Richard Tuffin, a 13-year-old schoolboy, set a record that still stands today when he was the cox for the New Zealand Coxed four as New Zealand's youngest ever competitor.

The Welsh town of Llanberis (pronounced 'Thlan-ber-ris') is on one side of the lake and makes an interesting stop off point. From the town you can take a train ride to the top of Mount Snowdon – or if you are feeling energetic, you can walk up. The Snowdon Race takes part annually in July, where competitors race to the top of the Mountain. It's five miles away and 3,560 feet up.

As well as the Snowdonia railway, you can also take the Llanberis Railway, which runs along the northern shores of Llyn Padarn. Look across the lake and think about the successful New Zealand rowers from 1958.

When in the area, take the opportunity to visit a Welsh castle. Mighty Caernarfon is only seven miles from Llanberis and is probably the most famous of the North Wales ring of castles.

The castle's construction began in 1283 and has acted not only as a military stronghold, but as a royal palace and as a seat of Government. This World Heritage site is truly majestic.

Millennium Stadium

Westgate Street, Cardiff, CF10 1NS
www.millenniumstadium.com

Ouch. The 2007 Rugby World Cup ended here in the Welsh capital as France came back from a 13-3 half-time deficit to beat the All Blacks 20-18.

The All Blacks first game at the newly built Millennium Stadium against South Africa also ended in defeat in an almost meaningless third place play-off as part of the 1999 World Cup. New Zealand were still reeling from the unbelievable second half comeback France had made the previous week in the semi-final at Twickenham.

Up until the 2011 Rugby World Cup, the All Blacks have beaten Wales on each of their seven encounters. In 2004 there was just a point in it 26-25, but two years later Wales were on the end of a 45-10 thrashing.

The stadium was built between 1997 and 1999 to replace Cardiff Arms Park. It is a spectacular stadium and has helped to revitalise Cardiff city centre. To make best use of the space, the stadium runs north south whereas the old Cardiff Arms Park ran east–west. The stadium has three tiers, can seat 74,500 and has a fully retractable roof, which can be opened or closed in just 20 minutes.

The retractable roof, its city centre location and the removable pitch system has put the Millennium Stadium on the map as being a world-class, must-visit, multi-event arena.

While the new Wembley Stadium was being built, the Millennium Stadium hosted rugby league Challenge Cup finals three times between 2003 and 2005. The stadium also hosted the Kiwis as part of the 2000 Rugby League World Cup. New Zealand beat Wales 58-18 in the group stages.

The stadium is owned by the Welsh Rugby Union and Wales play all their home matches here and the ground is also home to the Wales football team.

The stadium was home to all six FA Cup Finals between 2001 and 2006 while Wembley Stadium was under construction. Liverpool won the first and last of these finals while Arsenal took the title three times and Manchester United beat Millwall in 2004. The last final in 2006 when Liverpool beat West Ham on penalties has been dubbed the best Cup final of the modern era.

Local Welsh boxing hero Joe Calzaghe has fought twice at the Stadium in front of enormous crowds. He became the undisputed Super-Middleweight champion when he beat Mikel Kessler in front of 50,000 fellow Welshmen.

In 2005 the stadium hosted an indoor stage of the Rally Great Britain as part of the World Rally Championship and has welcomed the British Speedway Grand Prix for 12 years.

The stadium is a major concert venue for the world's biggest music superstars – U2, Madonna, Manic Street Preachers, Stereophonics, Robbie Williams, REM, Oasis, Paul McCartney and The Rolling Stones are among the acts to have played in the stadium.

In October 2011 the semi-final from the Rugby World Cup in New Zealand between Wales and France was shown on large screen TVs in the stadium. Over 62,000 people went to the stadium to see Wales lose 9-8. There was a bigger crowd here than those watching the actual match at Eden Park.

The stadium is in the heart of Cardiff and match days are great fun. The stadium is beside the River Taff and very near to Cardiff Central station. Welsh fans are always in good voice and there is traditionally good banter between sets of supporters. The Old Arcade is a traditional pub close to the ground and if you can get to the bar, it's a great place for a pint. Gwdihw is hard to pronounce but great to visit for a meal or to party afterwards.

Sophia Gardens Bowling Greens

Sophia Gardens, Cardiff, CF11 9SZ

This was the main bowling green, which hosted the Lawn Bowls at the 1958 British Empire and Commonwealth Games. New Zealand competed in the Singles, Pairs and Fours.

In the pairs' competition, John Morris and Richard Pilkington won 10 out of their 11 games to claim the top spot and the gold medal. They lost 21-12 to Rhodesia (modern day Zimbabwe) but won every other game.

New Zealand's James Pirrett could not repeat his gold medal winning performances from the Auckland games in 1950 or his silver medal in Vancouver four years later. He finished sixth winning six out of his 11 matches.

The New Zealand four finished 10th out of 12 teams winning just three games and losing eight.

Sophia Gardens is home to the Cardiff Bowling Club.

Stradey Park, Llanelli

Stradey Park (Now demolished): Isoced Road, Llanelli, SA15 4DA
Parc y Scarlets: Pemberton Park, Llanelli, SA14 9UZ
www.scarlets.co.uk

Halloween is traditionally the scariest day of the year and in 1972, the All Black's game on 31 October against Llanelli Scarlets at Stradey Park was a horror.

The Llanelli side claimed their greatest scalp with a *9-3* victory over New Zealand. The scoreboard read: 'Llanelli 9, Seland Newydd 3' and the 20,000 spectators and everyone else in town celebrated into the wee hours. It has been described by the locals ever since as 'the day the pubs ran dry'.

Welsh comedian and passionate rugby fan Max Boyce described the day in his song: 'And when I'm old, and my hair turns grey And they put me in a chair I'll tell my great-grandchildren that their Tad-cu, was there And they'll ask to hear the story Of that damp October day When I went down to Stradey And I saw the Scarlets play.'

New Zealand's only points that day came from the boot of full-back Joe Karam.

The Welsh team was so proud of the victory the scoreboard permanently showed this score when it was not otherwise in use during a match.

Even when the ground was being demolished in 2010, the scoreboard was moved to the replacement Parc y Scarlets stadium. According to their managing director: 'This is an important and very popular piece of our history that we will be taking with us to Parc y Scarlets. We wanted to ensure it is protected and admired by our supporters and visitors for years to come.'

New Zealand gained some measure of revenge in the Test a month later in 1972 at Cardiff Arms Park by beating Wales 19-16 but the match at Stradey Park went down in rugby history.

The stadium was demolished to make way for a housing development and a small memorial garden has been created to remember this great rugby pitch.

Swalec Stadium

(Formerly known as Sophia Gardens Cricket Ground)
Sophia Close, Cardiff, CF11 9XR
www.glamorgancricket.com

The SWALEC Stadium is a mile north of Cardiff Arms Park and is the home of Welsh cricket. Glamorgan County Cricket Club are based there and have successfully staged One-Day Internationals, Test Matches – including the First Test in the 2009 Ashes series – and major domestic finals including the Twenty20 finals day in 2012.

During the 1999 Cricket World Cup, New Zealand played at the ground, then known as Sophia Gardens, in the first-ever international one-day match at the ground (following the first phase of the ground development) when they beat Australia in the group stages.

On that day Canterbury's Geoff Allott took four wickets as the Black Caps restricted Australia to 213. New Zealand reached the target with more than four overs to spare thanks to an unbeaten 80 from Roger Twose and Chris Cairns who made 60.

New Zealand also beat the West Indies on the ground in 2004 as part of a triangular series with England.

Glamorgan is the only Welsh county side that is part of the England and Wales Cricket Board. The team has won the County Championship on three occasions – most recently in 1997.

Brendon McCullum and James Franklin both played for the county during the 2006 season and McCullum scored 160 on his debut against Leicestershire at Sophia Gardens.

The ground became known as the SWALEC Stadium in 2008, thanks to a sponsorship deal with a national electricity provider. It was previously known as Sophia Gardens – named after Sophia Rawdon-Hastings who was married to John Crichton Stuart who, as the Marquess of Bute, lived in Cardiff Castle and owned vast areas of land in the Welsh capital city, including the extensive area of Docks at the mouth of the River Taff.

A museum dedicated to the history and heritage of cricket in Wales is in the process of being created at the ground.

The Midlands

The east and west Midlands make up the heartland of England and this land-locked region is the country's industrial epicentre. The smog and factories of Birmingham and Wolverhampton contrast with the rural settings of Shropshire and Herefordshire.

Football teams from across the area have always been strong – Aston Villa and Nottingham Forest have both won European Cups while West Bromwich Albion, Birmingham City, Wolves, Coventry, Derby and Leicester have been in the Premier League in the past few years.

Across this region, cricket throughout the summer is hugely popular and the further south towards Leicestershire and Northamptonshire, rugby is more widely played.

Both Edgbaston and Trent Bridge are wonderful cricket venues and New Zealand supporters are always warmly welcomed.

Stratford-upon-Avon is a lovely town to visit and a great place to commemorate the works of Shakespeare; 400 years on and his writing is as inspirational today as ever.

Birmingham is England's second city and has recently undergone a renaissance through a redevelopment of its city centre shopping complex while the Peak district is beautiful and tranquil.

Every New Zealander should visit the town of Rugby – the cradle of the game is so important to the fabric of New Zealand.

The spa towns through the area are wonderful to visit and are always attractive to the eye. Towns such as Buxton and Royal Leamington Spa are worth a visit. One of the great attractions while travelling through the UK is to better understand our origins. Taste a Melton Mowbray Pork Pie in the town of the same name, know Hereford for more than the name of a cow breed or spot Robin Hood in the woods of Nottinghamshire.

Banks's Stadium

Address: Bescot Crescent, Walsall, WS1 4SA
www.saddlers.co.uk

Situated in the heart of the Midlands, often surrounded by smog, in the shadows of factories sits the English town of Walsall and its football stadium.

Within a stone's throw (if you can throw a stone 30 kilometres) are four more famous and more successful clubs, all which have regularly played football at the highest level – West Bromwich Albion, Birmingham City, Aston Villa and Wolverhampton Wanderers.

The team, nicknamed the Saddlers, were a founding member of the second division in 1892, but have never climbed to the top division.

Walsall moved into Banks's Stadium in 1990 (it is still better known by many as Bescot Stadium), having previously played at Fellows Park. The previous stadium has been demolished to make way for a Supermarket.

The club is famous for its proximity to one of Britain's busiest motorways – the M6 – and installing a large billboard advertisement that can be seen by up to 200,000 vehicles every day.

New Zealand footballer Danny Hay played 45 matches for Walsall after he left Leeds in 2002. Mark Paston who rose to New Zealand sporting fame at the World Cup in South Africa also played for Walsall for one season.

County Ground

The County Ground, Grandstand Road, Derby, DE21 6AF
www.derbyshireccc.com

Derbyshire County Cricket Club play their home matches on this ground –
often called the Racecourse as it formerly hosted horse racing meetings.

It used to be a football ground and Derby County played their matches here
until 1895 and in 1886, it became the first venue outside London to host
the FA Cup Final. Blackburn Rovers won their third consecutive trophy after
beating West Bromwich Albion 2-0 in the replay.

New Zealand has been involved in both of the international matches played
at the ground. Neither was a success. In the 1983 Cricket World Cup, New
Zealand lost to Sri Lanka and in 1999, they were beaten by Pakistan.

New Zealand does hold the record at the ground for the highest 50 overs
score when they made 369 against Derbyshire as a warm-up to the 1999
World Cup.

John Wright had a long and distinguished career at Derbyshire playing 156
matches between 1977 and 1988 and he scored over 10,000 runs at an
average of more than 44.

More recently, Martin Guptill played for the county side in 2011 and 2012.

Donington Race Track

Donington Park, Castle Donington, Derby, DE74 2RP
www.donington-park.co.uk

This race track in the heart of the East Midlands has hosted one Formula One
Grand Prix race but it is more famous as a motorcycle racing venue.

The 1993 European F1 Grand Prix was held here and Aryton Senna won
from Damon Hill. A memorial to Senna stands in the grounds of the track.

In 1986 New Zealander Richard Scott won the Donington International on
a 500cc Honda.

In 1997 New Zealand's Aaron Slight won the British round of the Superbikes

Racing down the hill at Donington during the British Touring Car Championships.

World Championship. A year later, compatriot Simon Crafar also claimed success on the track. He took the chequered flag in the 500cc British Grand Prix. This was Crafar's only ever Grand prix victory.

Donington is still home to the British round of the World Superbike Championships.

On four wheels the circuit hosts a round of the British Touring Car Championship as well as one of the European Le Mans Series rounds.

For fans of motor sport there is an excellent museum on site. The Donington Grand Prix Exhibition houses one of the largest collections of Grand Prix cars in the world. It is also home to the largest exhibition of McLaren and Williams Formula One Cars (outside of their respective factories).

You can bring your own car on specified dates and replicate Ayrton Senna as you race around Coppice corner at a Thunder in the Park Track Day at Donington Park.

Edgbaston

The County Ground, Edgbaston, Birmingham, B5 7QU
www.edgbaston.com

The cricket ground in central Birmingham has been New Zealand's least happy hunting ground in Test cricket.

In total, New Zealand have played four tests at Edgbaston each time resulting in a win to the home side.

Even when New Zealand beat England by two Tests to one, it was here that England won.

The 1958 New Zealand team were skittled by an English team including Fred Trueman and Jim Laker for 94 and 137.

The 1965 batsmen fared no better making only 116 in reply to England's 435 and were then always on the back foot.

In 1990, New Zealand drew at Trent Bridge and at Lord's but lost at Edgbaston. It was in this match where Sir Richard Hadlee played his last ever Test.

New Zealand's most successful ever series in England was a 2-1 victory in 1999. The series started auspiciously at Edgbaston. With a 100 run lead after the first innings, New Zealand crumbled to 52-8 but a late swashbuckling 46 from Simon Doull gave the tourists a degree of respectability finishing on 107. It was not to be enough. England reached their target with ease and the match was complete within three days. For England, Alex Tudor finished on 99 not out – his highest Test score.

New Zealand's one-day World Cup record over the years at the ground is much better. In 1975, New Zealand beat East Africa and in 1983 beat Pakistan and England. The 1999 World Cup team lost to South Africa.

One New Zealander to have achieved regular success at Edgbaston was Tom Pritchard who played for Warwickshire from 1946 until 1955. His quick bowling helped the County to championship victory in 1951. He is one of only four New Zealand born bowlers to have claimed more than 800 first class wickets (706 of these for Warwickshire at an average of 23.58). Ahead of him on that list are; Sir Richard Hadlee, Clarie Grimmet (who while born in New Zealand, played for Australia) and Sydney Smith.

Other notable New Zealanders who have played for Warwickshire include Martin Donnelly, Roger Twose, Don Taylor, Ray Hitchcock and Stew Dempster.

Renowned for having one of the best atmospheres in world cricket, Edgbaston completed a £32 million redevelopment project of its Pavilion End in the summer of 2011. The resulting new Pavilion Stand has increased capacity to 25,000 and made it the second biggest cricket ground in the UK behind Lord's.

Forest of Arden Golf Course

Maxstoke Lane, Meriden, Birmingham, CV7 7HR
www.marriottgolf.co.uk

This young parkland style course in Warwickshire was designed by Donald Steel and has hosted the British Masters and the English Open – both leading European Tour events.

It is a leading hotel and golf resort with a choice of restaurants, a spa and the leisure facilities you would expect from a leading hotel chain.

In 1997 New Zealand's Greg Turner shot 13 under par on his way to winning the One-2-One British Masters. Turner referenced the sponsor in his victory speech announcing his wife's pregnancy and that had been as a result of a 'one to one'. His older brother, renowned New Zealand poet Brian Turner, would have been pleased.

Turner won by one shot from Scotland's Colin Montgomerie. It was a close run thing as Turner played out from the bunker on the last hole to less than a metre from the pin to secure his par, the victory and a cheque for £125,000.

Holme Pierrepont

Adbolton Lane, Holme Pierrepont, Nottingham, NG12 2LU
www.nwscnotts.com

This exotically sounding Water Sports centre is five miles south of the city of Nottingham.

Set in a 270-acre park, the centre includes a six lane rowing course, a white water canoe slalom course and a lagoon for water-skiing. The Centre is open to the public and it can be an exhilarating weekend away or a relaxing stroll by the lake on a sunny afternoon.

The National Water Sports Centre also includes an indoor training hall – because you can never quite trust the British weather.

Holme Pierrepont's name derives from the old Danish word Holme meaning 'riverside meadow' while Pierrepont is the French family name of the family who owned the land since the 13th century.

The Centre has twice been host to the World Rowing Championships – firstly in 1975 and then again in 1986.

In 1975, the New Zealand Men's eight won a bronze medal – three years after their gold at the Munich Olympics.

In 1986 when the World Championships returned, the Men's Coxed four of Bruce Holden, Greg Johnston, Andrew Bird, Chris White and Nigel Atherfold won a silver medal while Stephanie Foster and Robyn Clarke won a bronze medal in the Women's Double Scull.

Jollees Cabaret Club, Stoke-on-Trent

Venue no longer exists
Approximate Address: Kingcross Street, Stoke-on-Trent, ST3 1NQ

From 1979 to 1985 this popular Stoke nightclub was host to the Darts World Championship.

The inaugural event was in Nottingham in 1978 but moved to Stoke a year later. Mike Watterson, a snooker promoter, came up with the idea of the World

Championship and with sponsorship from a tobacco firm and coverage on the BBC the event was off and running.

In the first year at Stoke, New Zealander Murray Smith lost 2-0 to Ireland's Jim McQuillan.

Through the 1970s and early 1980s audiences warmed to characters such as Bobby George, Jockey Wilson and John Lowe but it was Eric Bristow (nick-named the Crafty Cockney) whose skills and witty one liners turned the game into a worldwide sport.

Gordon Allpress was the only other New Zealander to compete in Stoke. He lost to Jocky Wilson in 1981 and to David Miller in 1982.

Apart from Darts, the venue was a Cabaret Club and hotspot for popular singers and comedians of the day. Cliff Richard, Tom Jones, Roy Orbison and Tommy Cooper all appeared here. One of the regular hosts was Pete Conway – better known as the father of singer Robbie Williams.

The nightclub eventually closed in the early 1990s and was eventually demolished. Building work began in 2004 and it is now home to a Wilkinson store.

Molineux Stadium, Wolverhampton

Waterloo Road, Wolverhampton, WV1 4QR
www.wolves.co.uk

Molineux is the home to football team Wolverhampton Wanderers – one of the founding clubs of the Football league – and it has been the club's home since 1889.

The club enjoyed most success between 1949 and 1960 under then manager Stan Cullis. In this time Wolves won three League titles and the FA Cup twice. Norman Deeley played on the wing for Wolves during this period, making 206 appearances and scoring 66 goals. He scored two goals in the 1960 FA Cup Final and was named Man of the Match. Deeley also played twice for England in 1959. His son Andy Deeley, played four times for the All Whites between 1986 and 1987 and scored six goals for New Zealand.

'Wolves' dress in orange and are supported by a fanatic fan-base. The atmosphere on a big match-day at Molineux is electric.

There are no pubs near the ground that welcome away supporters but the ground is only a 10-minute walk from the city centre, where you can get a pre match pint.

The club's darkest days were in the early and mid 1980s when the team sunk as low as the fourth division. It was during this time New Zealand's Rickie Herbert played for Wolves. The future All White coach played 49 games between 1984 and 1986. In both of these seasons, the club was relegated and Herbert returned to New Zealand soon afterwards.

National Indoor Arena

King Edward's Road, Birmingham, B1 2AA
www.thenia.co.uk

The National Indoor Arena in Birmingham is one of the UK's biggest and busiest large-scale indoor sporting and entertainment venues. Each year the venue hosts hundreds of events across sport, music, live theatre, comedy and family entertainment. The NIA has also hosted a range of international sporting events, from the World Trampolining and Tumbling Championships to the World Indoor Athletics, and has hosted the British Open Squash on three occasions.

In 1998 Paul Nicol from Scotland became the first man not named Khan to win the British Squash Open since 1981. All previous 16 titles had been won by Jahangir or Jansher Khan.

On the woman's side in an all Australian final, Michelle Martin beat Sarah Fitzgerald in a repeat of the 1996 and 97 finals.

In 2000, New Zealand's Leilani Joyce retained the title she had won the previous year in Aberdeen with a straight sets victory over England's Sue Wright. In the men's event, David Evans became the first ever Welsh champion as he beat Australian Paul Price.

The British Open is referred to as the Wimbledon of Squash and in 2001 the tournament returned to Birmingham. Sarah Fitzgerald won her first ever title having been runner-up three times before. She beat Carol Owens – an Australian at the time but who eventually became a New Zealand representative. Australian David Palmer won the men's competition – the last time Birmingham was host.

The National Indoor Arena also played host to the World Netball Championships in 1995. Where New Zealand finished third behind Australia and South Africa.

New Road Cricket Ground, Worcester

County Ground, New Road, Worcester, WR2 4QQ
www.wccc.co.uk

This pretty cricket ground in Worcester under the view of the Cathedral and surrounded by trees is home to the Worcestershire County Cricket side.

Arguably, New Zealand's finest batsman played for Worcestershire – Glenn Turner spent 14 seasons at New Road playing 284 first class matches.

In his time with the County he scored over 22,000 runs including one of

New Road – Worcestershire County Cricket Club with the cathedral in the background. (Picture: Ian Smith)

only three triple centuries ever scored on the ground.

He is still loved by cricket fans in the area – he was influential in the County's third Championship in 1974.

New Zealand's John Parker also played 61 matches for Worcestershire in the early 1970s.

Worcestershire has won the County Championship five times in total – most recently in 1989.

The New Zealand Women's cricket team have played three tests against England at New Road (on tours in 1954, 1984 and 1996) and all three matches ended in draws.

Because the ground is located next to the River Severn, the ground is prone to flooding, none more so than in 2007, when games had to be moved to other grounds in the county.

Northamptonshire County Cricket Ground

Abington Avenue, Northampton, NN1 4PR
www.northantscricket.com

This cricket ground in Northampton (also known as Wantage Road) is home to the County's cricket side and hosted the All Blacks when they played against the East Midlands on the 1924-25 Invincibles tour.

On 6 December 1925 16,000 people watched the All Blacks win their 23rd consecutive game on tour as the All Blacks won 31-7.

Numerous New Zealanders have played cricket for Northamptonshire – most notably four New Zealanders all played together for a time. Peter Arnold played from 1931 to 1940 while Ken James was with the club from 1935 through to 1939, Bill Merritt played in 1938 and in 1946 and Francis O'Brien played 40 matches during 1938 and 1939.

Much earlier than this, Sydney Smith played from 1907 through to 1914 and was club captain in the last two years. He was also voted as one of the five Wisden Cricketers of the Year for his 1914 season. Smith played cricket for both the West Indies early in his career and then New Zealand later in his career. His first match for New Zealand was against Australia in 1921.

Northamptonshire County Cricket Ground as viewed from the
Wantage Road End

Northamptonshire is one of only three sides (along with Gloucestershire and
Somerset) never to have won the County Championship.

Much more recently, Lou Vincent played a few games for the club during the
2010 season.

Up until 1994 Northampton Town FC also played at the ground but then
moved to Sixfields – a stadium designed specifically for football.

As with many other cricket grounds in England, it now also hosts concerts
and in 2011 you could have seen Elton John playing at the ground.

Rugby School

Rugby, Warwickshire, CV22 5EH
www.rugbyschool.net

It is on the playing fields of this exclusive school where William Webb Ellis allegedly caught the ball and ran with it hence creating New Zealand's national sport.

It may be a myth and a story but one that is important both to the game of
rugby and to New Zealand.

The story is in 1823, Ellis, then a pupil, cheated by catching the ball and
running forward with it.

The source of the information comes courtesy of a letter sent to the school by Matthew Bloxam in 1876 – four years after the death of Ellis and more than 50 years after the event. Bloxam, who was a solicitor, most likely received the information from one of his brothers, who was a contemporary of Ellis.

By the time investigations began in 1895 there was little first hand information available to go on. Some rugby historians now believe that Ellis may have been demonstrating the ancient Irish game of Caid as his father had spent a lot of time in Ireland.

What is certain is that Rugby School developed its own special rules of football which consequently led to the creation of the sport New Zealand now knows and loves.

Today the story lives on and William Webb Ellis is commemorated on a plaque at the school – as well as the World Cup trophy being named in his honour.

The plaque reads: 'This stone commemorates the exploit of William Webb Ellis who with a fine disregard for the rules of football as played in his time first took the ball in his arms and ran with it thus originating the distinctive feature of the rugby game AD 1823.'

All fans of the game should visit the town of Rugby, have a pint at the William Webb Ellis pub and raise a toast to the man who had a fine disregard for the rules of football.

Saffron Lane Velodrome, Leicester

Venue no longer exists
Approximate Address: Saffron Lane, Leicester, LE2 7NQ

The Saffron Lane Velodrome was built in 1969 in time to host the first international cycling championship in England a year later.

At those UCI Track Cycling World Championships, New Zealand's Harry Kent finished second in the Kilo time trial. In doing so, Kent became the first Kiwi cyclist to win a medal at this level.

Only a month after his Commonwealth Gold medal in Edinburgh, Kent finished second to Niels Fredborg from Denmark. Kent came home to New

Zealand to the plaudits and won the Lonsdale Cup and was the Halberg Sportsperson of the year.

When first built, Saffron Lane was a concrete track, but in 1978 the track was relaid with wooden boards and it again hosted the World Championships in 1982.

Over the years, the venue fell into disrepair and since the Millennium there was no racing as the wood had rotted away. In 2008, the council demolished the Velodrome, as the site had become a danger to the public.

Silverstone

Towcester, Northamptonshire, NN12 8TN
www.silverstone.co.uk

In rural Northamptonshire, the home of British Formula One was born from an unneeded World War Two airfield. The first Formula One Grand Prix race at the track was in 1948 and Silverstone was the host every second year until 1986 when it became the sole permanent host.

Originally a farm was in the centre of the Silverstone track and the wheat was usually at its highest for the July race.

While no New Zealander has ever won a Formula One race in the UK, in 1967 Denny Hulme finished second behind Jack Brabham. That was the year Hulme became World Champion. In that same race, Chris Amon finished third and Bruce McLaren retired.

While Bruce McLaren retired in the 1967 race, he had previously been on the podium in 1959 and was again in 1969.

Four New Zealanders competed at Silverstone in 1973. Denny Hulme finished third, Howard Ganley finished ninth and Chris Amon retired. The other New Zealander in the field was Graham McRae – he retired on the first lap in his only ever start in a Formula One. This is one of the shortest Formula One careers of all time.

The grandstand at Stowe corner is one of the great sporting seats in the UK – even more so when a British driver is doing well in the championship. Cars roar down Hangar Straight braking on the corner immediately in front of you.

It was at this corner where Nigel Mansell took the lead from teammate Nelson Piquet in 1987 with just two laps remaining having come back from 28 seconds behind. The partisan fans cheered and cheered and Mansell only just had enough fuel to get to the finish. He ran out on the slowing down lap and was mobbed by overjoyed fans in what is considered one of the greatest Formula One races ever.

Tragically, New Zealand motorcyclist Kim Newcombe died at Stowe corner while racing in 1973. Despite not racing in the last two races, he posthumously finished second in the World 500cc Grand Prix standings. In 2005 an award winning television documentary called *Love, Speed and Loss* was made about Newcombe.

The Hawthorns

Halford's Lane, West Bromwich, West Midlands, B71 4LF
www.wba.co.uk

This is the home ground of English football team, West Bromwich Albion, who are better known to British football supporters as the Baggies.

The ground's name is derived from the Hawthorn bushes, which needed to be cleared to make way for the new stadium when it was built for the 1900-01 season.

The ground is famous for two things – firstly it is the highest ground in the Football League in terms of altitude and it was the last stadium to have been built in the 19th-century.

While the team was one of the founding members of the Football League, they have won the League only once – the 1919-20 season. The club has also won the FA Cup five times, most recently in 1968 when they beat Everton 1-0.

Over the past decade the club has yo-yoed between the Premier League and the second flight Championship.

The Birmingham Road End stand at the ground is where the most passionate supporters sit and where the most singing in the ground comes from. The club are well known for singing Psalm 23 – The Lord's My Shepherd.

New Zealand striker Chris Wood with West Bromwich Albion.

The club used to be known as the Throstles and it was one of these song-birds which used to adorn the team's emblem. (The bird is better known in New Zealand as a song thrush.) It was chosen by the club because the local pub where the team used to get changed before games kept one in a cage as a pet.

Today, one of the best places to have a drink before or after the game is at The Vine, where the pub also serves delicious Indian food.

Chris Wood from Hamilton, New Zealand joined the Baggies and made his first team debut in April 2009 and became only the fifth New Zealander to play in the Premier League. Wood was part of the All White squad that travelled to South Africa for the World Cup Finals.

Tour of Britain

www.thetour.co.uk

The Tour of Britain criss-crosses the country in a different route each year and is one of the bigger cycle tours in Europe.

It is not on the same level as the Tour de France, the Giro d'Italia or La Vuleta but it is growing in stature and importance since the race was revived in 2004.

Historically, the British national tour was known as the Milk Race due to sponsorship from the Milk Marketing Board. Between 1945 and 1984 it was strictly for amateurs but professionals could enter after this date, with the race lasting until 1993. A professional race, the Kellogg's tour ran from 1987 to 1994 and then as the PruTour for 1998-99 until funding dried up.

Since The Tour of Britain was revived in 2004, the race has become a stop on the UCI European calendar – it takes place in September towards the end of the season. In that first year, New Zealand's Julian Dean finished in second place and won the Points jersey.

New Zealand's Greg Henderson finished third for Team Sky in the 2010 Tour and also won the Points Jersey. He won the second stage that year around Stoke-on-Trent.

Previously, New Zealanders have experienced success on the tour. In

New Zealand's Greg Henderson winning Stage 2 of the
Tour of Britain in 2010.

1988, Graeme Millar won two stages on the 1988 Kellogg's Tour while in
1977 Roger Sumich won the Tour's first stage. One of New Zealand's earliest
competitors in the race was British Empire and Commonwealth Games double
bronze medallist Warwick Dalton who won two stages in 1961.

Trent Bridge

Trent Bridge, Nottingham, NG2 6AG
www.nottsccc.co.uk

Trent Bridge is viewed by many commentators as one of the finest cricket
grounds in the world.

It dates back to the 1830s when they fenced off land at the back of the pub
to start playing cricket. In 1899 it hosted its first international match making it
the world's third oldest Test ground.

Trent Bridge is home to Nottinghamshire County Cricket Club. The team
has won the County Championship six times in its history and a number of
New Zealanders have played for Notts.

Recently, Stephen Fleming captained Notts to County Championship glory in 2005. Other New Zealanders who have played for the county include Chris Cairns, Daniel Vettori and Nathan Astle. In the 2010 season Andre Adams claimed the most wickets in County cricket to help Notts to a sixth title.

All were following in the footsteps of Sir Richard Hadlee who was part of championship winning sides in 1981 and 1987. Hadlee played for 10 seasons at Notts but due to injuries and Test commitments 1981, 84 and 87 were the only three seasons he played a full part. Hadlee's figures in those two championship-winning seasons are beyond reproach. In 1981 he took 105 wickets at an average of 14.89 and in 1987 he took 97 wickets at an even more astounding average of 11.89. In 1984 he did the County double by taking 100 wickets (at 14.05) and scoring 1000 runs.

Trent Bridge will always live long in New Zealand's sporting history. It was victory on this ground in 1986 that would give the team its first Test series victory on English soil.

Not surprisingly, Sir Richard Hadlee was at the heart of that famous win. He starred with the ball taking six wickets and then with the bat, scoring 68 and steadying the ship when New Zealand was teetering at 144-5. He took another four wickets in the second innings to give him 10 for the match. New Zealand made the 73 for victory with ease and unsurprisingly Hadlee was named man of the match.

Previously, Hadlee played his second ever Test match in June 1973 and in an amazing match in which New Zealand made 97 in their first innings and

Trent Bridge is a beautiful ground to watch cricket.

were chasing an unlikely 479 for victory. At 402–5 it looked good but the tail collapsed and came up 38 runs short.

New Zealand has played five World Cup one-day matches at Trent Bridge. In 1999, New Zealand beat India in the Super Sixes en route to the semi-final. New Zealand will play one-day games at Trent Bridge against England on both their 2013 and 2015 tours.

Victoria Park Bowling Green

Archery Road, Leamington Spa, Warwickshire, CV31 3PT
www.warwickdc.gov.uk

The Victoria Park Bowling Green was the home to the 2004 Women's World Championship after it was moved from Malaysia.

The home of Women's bowling in England, also hosted the 1996 World Championship and since 1974 has been the venue for the English National Championship.

In 2004 New Zealand's Jo Edwards and Sharon Sims teamed up to win the Pairs competition. Two years earlier, the pair had won gold at Manchester at the Commonwealth Games.

Their success at Royal Leamington Spa brought them a nomination for Team of the Year in the Halberg awards but they lost out to the Evers-Swindell twins.

Royal Leamington Spa is within 10 miles of Stratford-Upon-Avon. This popular town is famed as the birthplace of William Shakespeare, who apparently, was a bowler. He wrote about bowls on numerous occasions such as in Richard II.

Shakespeare writing Richard II act 3 scene 4, sets the scene at Langley in the garden of the Duke of York. Enter the Queen and two Ladies.

Queen – 'What sport shall we devise here in this garden, to drive away the heavy thought of care.'

Lady – 'Madam, we'll play at bowls.'

Queen – ''Twill make me think the world is full of rubs, And that my fortune rubs against the bias.'

You can play on the bowling green as a casual player. In 2012 the cost per person was £4 per hour.

Villa Park, Birmingham

Trinity Road, Birmingham, B6 6HE
www.avfc.co.uk

Villa Park in Birmingham is home to Premier League side Aston Villa and has twice hosted the All Blacks on visits to the UK.

Aston Villa have spent over 100 years in total in the top flight of English football (second only to Everton) and have won both the League Championship and the FA Cup each seven times. The Villains are also one of only five English sides to have won the European Cup, after beating Bayern Munich 1-0 in the 1982 final. Peter Withe was the goalscoring hero that night.

The two most important days of the year for fans are games with cross-town rivals Birmingham City and these are always fiercely contested.

The ground itself is one of the most highly rated football stadia in the UK and has hosted numerous international and high profile matches such as England games, 1966 World Cup games and FA Cup semi-finals.

As well as football, the All Blacks have twice played at Villa Park. Most recently in 1953 when the All Blacks beat a Midland Counties side 18-3.

On the 1924-25 Invincibles Tour Jim Parker scored five tries helping the men in black beat a North Midlands XV by 40-3. Possibly one of the most romantic All Blacks – it was Parker who combined the early part of this same tour to Australia with his honeymoon. He then continued onto the UK while his bride returned to New Zealand.

Welford Road

Aylestone Road, Leicester, LE2 7TR
www.leicestertigers.com

Welford Road is the venue where the All Blacks have played the most rugby matches in England away from Twickenham.

The All Blacks have played 14 matches at Welford Road in Leicester – one Test during the 1991 World Cup against Italy and 13 tour matches.

In 1991 the All Blacks beat Italy 31-21 and have lost only one of the tour matches – against the Midland Division on 8 November 1983. Outside of Test matches, this loss is one of only eight tour games the All Blacks have ever lost in the UK.

The match versus Italy was the All Black's final group game of the 1991 World Cup. They went on to beat Canada in the quarter-final before losing to Australia in the semi-final in Dublin.

As well as the 1991 World Cup match, Italy lost to Tonga in the 1999 World Cup; Welford Road is one of the grounds selected for the 2015 Rugby World Cup when it returns to England.

Welford Road is the home to Leicester rugby and New Zealanders who have played at the club include Josh Kronfeld, Daryl Gibson and Aaron Mauger as well as Ernest Booth who was on the 1905 Originals Tour.

More recently, Craig Newby, Scott Hamilton and Thomas Waldrom have all played at Welford Road for the Leicester Tigers.

Since rugby became professional, Leicester Tigers have been a powerhouse in the Premiership with seven league titles and have twice won the Heineken European Cup.

The North West

The North West of England is dominated by two rival major cities – Liverpool and Manchester.

Liverpool grew rich through the 18th-century with the city's port accounting for up to 40 per cent of the world's trade by the end of the century. It was also the last port of call for immigrants heading to the fledgling USA.

This wealth can still be seen today in the exquisite waterfront buildings such as The Royal Liver Building, the Cunard Building and The Port of Liverpool Building – together known as the Three Graces. The creation of the shipping canal as well as a new railway line to Manchester from Liverpool made Manchester the centre for the surrounding cotton spinning towns (such as Bury and Oldham and Bolton) and. the town grew incredibly wealthy as a result through the mid 1800s.

Both Liverpool and Manchester were targets for the German bombers in World War Two and both towns suffered significant damage.

Liverpool's music scene boomed in the 1960s led by The Beatles and the city is still rightly proud of the 'Fab Four'. The Cavern on Matthew Street in Liverpool where the band became famous has been recreated and you can go along at any time and sing along.

Manchester's music scene reached its most heady days in the 80s and then the 90s with bands such as The Happy Mondays and The Stone Roses followed by New Order and Oasis.

On the football field, the rivalry is at its most intense. Liverpool versus Manchester United is one of the most-anticipated matches of the season.

While in the cities, music was to the forefront – economically both cities were beginning to lag behind the rest of the nation. In Manchester, it took a tragedy to create the necessary renaissance. An IRA bomb rocked the city in 1996 and led to a redevelopment of the city centre.

Liverpool's nadir came in 1981 as race riots rocked the city. But it was not until 2003 when Liverpool was awarded European Capital of Culture for 2008 that the city was redeveloped to its former glory.

Away from Liverpool and Manchester surrounding industrial towns (such as Wigan and St Helens) are hotbeds for rugby league while numerous courses make the area known as England's Golf Coast. Royal Liverpool and Birkdale both host the Open but from a New Zealand perspective it was at Royal Lytham just outside Blackpool where Bob Charles became Open Champion in 1963.

Aintree Motor Racing Circuit – Liverpool

Melling Road, Aintree, Liverpool, L9 0LQ
www.liverpoolmotorclub.com

While the Aintree name may be better known for its horse racing track as the site for the Grand National, the Motor Racing circuit hosted the British Grand Prix five times in the 1950s and 1960s.

At the time there were two tracks situated within the horse racing track and used the same grandstands. In 1957 over 150,000 spectators watched the Grand Prix action.

It was here that New Zealand's Bruce McLaren finished third in 1959 and eighth in 1961. In 1962 McLaren was again on the podium, finishing third behind Jim Clark and John Surtees.

In this same race, New Zealander Tony Shelly qualified for his only ever Grand Prix start but retired just six laps into the race.

The full circuit was last raced on in 1964 and today only the Club circuit remains within the horse racing track. Through the year there is a limited amount of motor racing organised including car sprints and motorcycle racing as well as track days for the general public.

Within the Club circuit, there is a 9-hole public golf course, which is very reasonably priced and gives you the chance to step where legends have raced (whether that was four hooves or four wheels).

Aintree Racecourse

Ormskirk Road, Aintree, Liverpool, L9 5AS
www.aintree.co.uk

This is the home of the race that stops the nation. The Grand National is held in April and brings the jumps season to a close.

The Aintree track is in north Liverpool, and the locals love to host a party. There are over 70,000 people on the course and they are all cheering. The race is one of the highlights of the British sporting calendar. Tickets go on sale in August and many Grand Stand badges sell out almost immediately.

Action from the Grand National Festival at Aintree.

The noise on course when the race starts is incredible. As well as the huge crowds on course, every year 500 to 600 million people tune in to watch the race on TV in over 140 countries.

The race is four miles, four furlongs (or just over 7.2 kms) and the horses jump 30 fences. It is one of racing's greatest challenges – a unique test of horse and rider. Only once this millennium, have more than half the horses that started, managed to finish.

The Chair and Becher's Brook are the two most famous fences on the track. Becher's Brook has been previously described by jockeys like 'jumping off the edge of the world'.

It is the most popular race in the UK and for some armchair punters it is their only bet of the year. The only betting tip we can offer is to avoid the grey horses. The race at Aintree dates back to 1839 and in that time only three greys have ever won – The Lamb in 1868 and 1871, Nicholas Silver in 1961 and most recently, Neptune Collonges in 2012.

The winning horse and jockey become the nation's darlings and the most famous winner of all is Red Rum. With back-to-back wins in 1973 and 74, and second places in 1975 and 1976, he was considered too old in 1977. In a race when only nine of the 42 horses finished, Red Rum won by 25 lengths and became the first horse to win the great race three times.

'Rummy' was trained on the sands at nearby Southport by Liverpool's Ginger McCain. Red Rum died in 1995 and is buried by the winning post at Aintree.

A memorial reads: "Respect this place / this hallowed ground / a legend here / his rest has found / his feet would fly / our spirits soar / he earned our love for evermore."

In a 2007 poll, it was found Red Rum was still the most well-known horse in British racing.

The unluckiest story of Aintree belongs to Devon Loch in 1956. Fewer than 50 yards from the finish and five lengths ahead, the horse mysteriously did a half jump and belly-flopped down on to the ground, landing on its stomach. ESB took over and won in the most remarkable finish to a horse race. Devon Loch was owned by Queen Elizabeth the Queen Mother and she famously said: 'Oh, that's racing.'

New Zealand horses have traditionally done well at Aintree. Moifaa won the Grand National in 1904. The horse was bred and raced in New Zealand before moving to the UK. A myth surrounds the horse that he swam for safety after a shipwreck and was found the next day.

The reality is that it was another New Zealand horse Kiora who swam for two miles after a shipwreck off Cape Hope and competed against Moifaa in 1904. The myth developed from this coincidence.

After his Grand National triumph, Moifaa was bought by King Edward VII, became the monarch's favourite horse and led the King's funeral procession in 1910.

In 1991 New Zealand bred horse Seagram won the race. Seagram was bred in Waikato by Jeanette Broome at Loch Haven Thoroughbred, who also bred 1998 Melbourne Cup winner Jezabeel.

New Zealand's Lord Gyleene won the Grand National in 1997. It is the only year that the race has been held on a Monday – because of an IRA bomb threat on the scheduled Saturday. The course was immediately evacuated and thousands of people were unable to return to their cars to fetch their belongings. With insufficient hotel accommodation in the immediate area, generous Liverpudlians opened their homes to the race-going public.

New Zealand horse Royal Mail raced three times between 1981 and 1983 – finishing third in 1981 behind Aldaniti and Spartan Missile.

There was a New Zealand link for the 1987 winner – Maori Venture. The horse was named after its breeder Dai 'Maori' Morgan – who was affectionately nicknamed from his time playing rugby in New Zealand.

Two famous films are set around The Grand National. *Champions* is about jockey Bob Champion who recovered from cancer to win the 1981 race aboard Aldaniti.

National Velvet shot Elizabeth Taylor to stardom when it was made in 1944. Taylor starred in this Oscar winning film as the jockey trying to win the Grand National. Taylor was ahead of her time – the first female jockey was Charlotte Brew in 1977.

Grand National Day at Aintree is one of the great days on the British sporting calendar and a must-do for any sports fan.

Anfield

Anfield Road, Liverpool, L4 0TH
www.liverpoolfc.com

One of the things many sports fans travelling to the UK find different from New Zealand sports venues is that singing is a key component of going to the match.

Whether this is at Twickenham, where the English crowd sings 'Swing Low Sweet Chariots'; 'Marching on together at Leeds' or 'Comin' home Newcastle' some songs are synonymous with some teams.

But, from the home city of the Beatles, without doubt the most famous song in football is Liverpool's, You'll Never Walk Alone, which the crowd sing before the start of every match at Anfield.

For first timers to Anfield, it is the moment they will never forget having been to the famous ground. As the fans hold their scarves above their heads the hairs on the back of the neck prickle and, if you're lucky enough to be in the heart of the Kop stand, life feels very special indeed.

Ironically, the song comes from a 1940s Rodgers and Hammerstein musical – Carousel. It was covered by Merseyside band Gerry and the Pacemakers in the 1960s and quickly became an anthem sung by fans. The song is so intrinsically linked to the club that it is part of the logo, and is on the Shankly Gate entrance to the stadium.

Liverpool is one of the great football teams in the world. With 18 championships, seven FA Cups and five European Cups they have one of the best records in sport, but Liverpool is more than just what happens on the pitch. The team is a global brand with heart, soul and spirit.

The team has twice been involved in stadium disasters. At Heysel, 39 Juventus fans died and this resulted in English sides being banned from playing in Europe.

At Sheffield Wednesday's Hillsborough Stadium in 1989, 96 Liverpool fans died after being crushed at the Leppings Lane end of the ground at an FA Cup match with Nottingham Forest. The subsequent Taylor Report named the failure of police control. There is a memorial at Anfield to those who died on the day.

Liverpool FC was formed in 1892 by John Houlding after a dispute about land with fellow local side Everton who were playing at Anfield at the time. Everton moved across Stanley Park to Goodison Park, and Liverpool was formed and the club made Anfield their home. The stadia are within a mile of each other and the rivalry between the two sides has existed ever since.

The rivalry is slightly friendlier than other cross-city rivalries, such as Manchester, Glasgow or Birmingham.

Legendary Liverpool manager, Bill Shankly may disagree. He once said the two best teams in the city were Liverpool and Liverpool Reserves. He also said: 'If Everton were playing at the bottom of the garden, I'd pull the curtains.' There is a statue outside the Anfield ground in his honour.

Two (eventual) New Zealanders signed for Liverpool, but never played in the first team. Phil Dando was a goalkeeper and signed for Liverpool in 1969 under Bill Shankly. He played at Barrow and Bury before moving to New Zealand where he played two games for the All Whites.

Billy McClure played for Liverpool reserves between 1974 and 1977. He moved to Auckland in 1979 and played for the All Whites between 1981 and 1986. He was a member of the All White squad at the World Cup in 1982 in Spain.

The All Blacks played at Anfield in 1993 when they beat a North of England selection 27-21. Eric Rush scored one of New Zealand's tries to the delights of the journalists, as Ian Rush was a hero to Liverpool football followers.

Rugby will return to Anfield as the stadium has been chosen to stage group games when England hosts the 2015 World Cup.

Birkenhead Park

The Upper Park, Park Road North, Birkenhead, CH41 8AA.
www.birkenheadparkrugby.co.uk

Across the River Mersey from Liverpool is Wirral. This peninsula, hemmed in by the Rivers Dee and Mersey, is rich in Norse Viking history.

If you are visiting Liverpool, take the famous ferry across the river, admire the city's wonderful architecture from the water and sing along to *Ferry across the Mersey.* When in Wirral, visit Royal Liverpool Golf Club, which will host the 2014 British Open and visit Birkenhead Park which was the country's first publically funded park and an inspiration for Frederick Olmsted's design of New York's Central Park.

The rugby club at Birkenhead Park plays in the equivalent of the fifth division of 12 in English rugby. However, the ground has hosted the All Blacks four times – firstly in 1905 on the Originals tour and most recently in 1978.

In 1905 the All Blacks won 34-0. The Liverpool Courier wrote of the match: 'Individually the All Blacks were incomparably superior. Collectively, they were ridiculously superior.'

The ground is a good indication of how English rugby put together stronger and stronger sides over the years to try and beat the All Blacks. In 1905 and 1924, the All Blacks played county side, Cheshire. Then in 1935, it was a combined side from Lancashire and Cheshire but this finished 21-8 to the New Zealanders.

The last time the All Blacks played at Birkenhead Park was in 1978 against a North of England team and New Zealand won 9-6 on the day watched by a crowd of over 10,000.

Birkenhead Park was also used as part of the RFU Centenary celebrations in 1971 when a crowd of 10,000 watched the North of England play a World XV whose squad included such famous All Blacks as Brian Williams, Sid Going, Ian Kirkpatrick, Brian Lochore and Colin Meads.

Bloomfield Road

Seasiders Way, Blackpool, Lancashire, FY1 6JJ
www.blackpoolfc.co.uk

This is the home ground of football side, Blackpool. The team known as the Seasiders (for geographic reasons) or as the Tangerines (for their bright tangerine strip) have played at the ground since 1901. The club's heyday was in the 1950s when members of the squad, such as Stanley Matthews, were playing for England. Blackpool's best finish in the League was in 1955-56 when they finished second in the League to Manchester United.

Blackpool lifted the FA Cup in 1953 and while Stan Mortensen may have scored a hat-trick in the final it became known as the 'Matthews final' as it was the 'Wizard of Dribble' who inspired his team to come back from 3-1 down with 20 minutes to go to win 4-3 with an extra-time goal.

Decline followed and by the start of the 70s the club was back in the lower divisions and by the end of the 1980s Blackpool were playing in England's Fourth Division.

Since the turn of the millennium, Blackpool have made a comeback, culminating with their promotion to the Premier League in May 2010 when they beat Cardiff City in the Play-off final. They were subsequently relegated after their first year in the top-flight.

One New Zealand born footballer has played for Blackpool. Jon Rush was born in Wellington but returned to the UK when very young. He progressed through football's youth systems and became a professional at Blackpool and played 13 league games for the team in the early 1980s.

Steve Sumner captained New Zealand's All Whites at the World Cup in Spain in 1982 but was born and bred in the Lancashire region and was an apprentice pro at Blackpool and at Preston before moving to New Zealand.

Central Park, Wigan

Stadium no longer exists
Approximate Address: Central Park Way, Wigan, WN1 1XS

Wigan has always been a rugby league town and Central Park was home from 1903 until 1999 when the team moved to ground-share at the JJB Stadium.

For the first six years the changing rooms were at the nearby Prince of Wales pub, but changes were made to the ground throughout its life. In 1959 almost 50,000 spectators packed into the ground to watch the derby with St Helens. This stood as a League record attendance for over 40 years.

But as ground safety regulations increased and there were more seats, rather than terraces, the maximum attendance fell.

Wigan Warriors celebrated 17 League titles, a Super League title (1998) and 16 Challenge Cup wins while at the ground. As Wigan became the most famous team in rugby league, Central Park, became one of the most famous grounds in the sport.

Billy Boston is the most famous player for the club. He played 488 games for the club over 15 years and scored 478 tries. The Billy Boston Stand, built in 1991, was named in his honour and it proved to be an endearing landmark for the stadium. When the club moved to the JJB Stadium a stand there was named in his honour.

The height of Wigan's glory years were the late 1980s and 1990s as the team won nearly every honour on offer. Between 1988 and 1997, the team won the League eight times, the Challenge Cup nine times, the premiership trophy six times and the World Club Challenge three times.

New Zealanders were the heartbeat of this success. Graham Lowe coached the team from 1986 to 1989. Graeme West took the reins from 1994 to 1997. Dean Bell played over 250 games between 1986 and 1994 and was named the team's Hall of Fame. Other New Zealanders who starred in these years included Graeme West, Tony and Kevin Iro, Adrian Shelford, Frano Botica and Inga Tuigamala.

Many New Zealanders have played for Wigan over the years, dating back to Lance Todd (between 1908 and 1913) for whom the Man of the Match trophy in the Challenge Cup Final is named after.

Todd was ahead of his time. In 1931, as manager of Salford he wanted to move rugby league to a summer season and said, 'Of course, we shall hear that summer is the cricket season, but by what divine right was it allocated to cricketers?' Rugby league did eventually switch successfully to a summer season – in 1996.

One teammate of Lance Todd was Charlie Seeling, a member of the 1905 All Blacks, who signed for Wigan in 1910. He played over 200 games and is in the New Zealand Sports Hall of Fame. His son Charlie Seeling (Junior) also went on to play for Wigan.

New Zealander Ces Mountford was the first non-Englishman to win The Lance Todd Trophy in 1951. He played 210 games for Wigan, coached the Kiwis and was elected into the New Zealand Sports Hall of Fame – but he never played for the national side.

Massa Johnston toured with both the All Blacks in 1905 and with the All Golds in 1907-08 and signed for Wigan soon afterwards.

Len Mason played over 360 games for Wigan and Arthur Francis made over 200 appearances for the team.

The Kiwis played Great Britain six times at Central Park, but never won. They beat France in the 1960 World Cup but were thrashed 47-11 in the 1970 World Cup by Australia.

The last game at Central Park was September 1999 in an emotional match against old rival St Helens that saw hardened rugby league fans weep.

It was demolished soon afterwards and is now a car park for a major super-market. There is a monument, commemorating where the ground used to stand.

DW Stadium

Loire Drive, Wigan, WN5 0UZ
www.wiganwarriors.com and www.wiganlatics.co.uk

This is the only ground in the country that is home to a Premier League team and a top-flight rugby league team. Wigan Athletic and Wigan Warriors both call the ground their home.

Wigan Warriors moved to the ground after they emotionally left Central Park in 1999.

Wigan Athletic had previously played at Springfield Park, which has now been demolished to make way for a housing development. Since the team have moved to the ground Wigan has gone from the third tier of English football to the high table of the Premier League.

The stadium is named after DW Sports Fitness – a company owned by Dave Whelan who owns both Wigan Athletic and the ground itself. Whelan also formerly owned Wigan Warriors but sold the club in 2007.

Wigan is the most successful team in British rugby league. Many New Zealanders have played and coached at the Warriors while the team has been at the DW Stadium. Frank Endacott coached the side in their first two seasons at the new stadium until he was sacked in 2001.

Quentin Pongia, Jerry Seuseu, David Vaealiki, Iafeta Paleaaesina and Jeff Lima are among the New Zealanders who have played for the Cherries over the past decade at the DW Stadium.

The most famous New Zealander to have played for Wigan recently is Thomas Leuluai who helped New Zealand to win the World Cup over Australia in 2007. He marshalled Wigan to win the Challenge Cup in 2011 and the Super League Grand final in 2010 where he was Man of the Match.

Wigan Athletic has flourished since moving to the ground. They have generally been in the bottom half of the Premier League but up to 2012/2013 have not been relegated in the eight seasons since they were promoted. Founded in 1932, this is the first time the club has reached the top flight of the English game.

But, while Wigan Athletic and the Wigan Warriors share a ground, there is no shared love between supporters – it is animosity. There have been issues between the two teams over the ground – in 2008 the Warriors were forced to play a Super League Play-off match at nearby Widnes because the football side was already scheduled to play at the DW Stadium.

The stadium is near the canal and a shopping complex. If you are driving, it is better not to park at the Supermarket as cars are regularly clamped and the release fee is expensive.

If you are visiting Wigan then have a drink at the George Orwell Pub. It's not often you can combine literature and sport in an afternoon. It's a fair walk to the ground from there but you can nod your cap to the man who wrote The Road to Wigan Pier. It's a book that focuses upon how the working class in the northern industrial areas of England lived through the great depression of the 1930s. It's something to think about as you walk to the ground, like millions have done before you.

Etihad Stadium

(Formerly The City of Manchester Stadium)
SportCity, Manchester, M11 3FF
www.mcfc.co.uk

This is the home of Premier League football team, Manchester City but it was built to host the 2002 Commonwealth Games.

The Commonwealth Games in Manchester had a more profound effect on the city and on the nation as a whole then just winning or losing gold medals. By the end of the 1990s Great Britain had become a sporting lightweight on the world stage – the 2005 World Athletics Championships had to be moved away from the UK, after the country broke promises about delivering a new stadium. Within the sporting world, the country was developing a reputation for failed projects and broken promises.

The City of Manchester Stadium had been damaged by a 1996 IRA bombing and the Games heralded a new start.

Sportcity was at the heart of this regeneration. The City of Manchester stadium was the sparkling jewel within this crown. The games were a roaring success – not just from a sporting perspective, but from a local and national perspective.

The Games helped to restore Britain's reputation on the world stage. The organisers of the London 2012 Olympic bid owe a debt of gratitude to the city of Manchester.

Sport has enhanced the life of the city and the lives of those in the city. Ten years on, people are now wondering if Manchester, not Birmingham, is in fact England's second city.

New Zealanders marched at the stadium in the Opening and Closing ceremonies. Cyclist Sarah Ulmer carried the flag at the Opening ceremony while weightlifter Neil Avery carried it at the Closing ceremony celebrating his two gold medals.

It was here that the athletics took place and Beatrice Faumuina won her second Commonwealth gold medal in the women's discus with a throw of 60.83 metres.

It was here that Valerie Adams tasted her first senior success – finishing second in the Women's Shot Put. Craig Barrett finished second in the Men's 50km walk and Philip Jensen threw the Hammer 69.48 metres to win a silver medal.

On the final day of competition in the Rugby sevens and just like in Malaysia four years earlier, New Zealand was triumphant. The All Blacks beat Fiji 33-15 in the final. A seemingly comfortable score-line but with 30 seconds to go, New Zealand trailed by a point. Craig de Goldi scored and then Bruce Reihana and Roger Randle both dotted down in injury time to make the gold medal safe.

When Manchester City moved to the stadium from Maine Road in August 2003, the team had just won promotion from the lower divisions.

Fans are again dreaming of glory – not seen since the 1960s and 70s when the club won the League, FA Cup and European Cup Winners' Cup under legendary Manager Joe Mercer.

In 2011, the club won the FA Cup by beating Stoke City in the final. In May 2012 Manchester City won the Premier League on the final day of the season with a goal in extra-time, beating cross-town rival Manchester United into second place.

Ewood Park

Ewood Park, Blackburn, BB2 4JF
www.rovers.co.uk

Home to Blackburn Rovers, this ground was where New Zealand's Ryan Nelsen made his name in English football.

The gritty defender joined the club in January 2005 and played 208 times for the club before leaving for Tottenham Hotspur in February 2012.

Throughout Nelsen's time at the club, Blackburn Rovers was in the Premier League but were relegated after Nelsen left.

In 1992 English football changed from the First Division to become the Premier League. In those years, only five teams won the title – both Manchester teams, Arsenal, Chelsea and Blackburn Rovers, who won the title in 1995.

Blackburn is one of the founding members of the Football League and has won the FA Cup six times – the last time was in 1928.

Rovers are the longest serving team who have played at one ground – Ewood Park has been home since 1890. The club's most intense rivalry is with neighbouring Burnley.

Ewood Park also played host to the Kiwis in 2002 when they won 30-16 over Great Britain in a rugby league international.

Haliwell Jones Stadium

Mike Gregory Way, Warrington, WA2 7NE
www.warringtonwolves.com

In 2007 to celebrate the centenary of the All Golds rugby league tour to the UK, a one-off match between a New Zealand side and a Northern Union side took place at this Warrington stadium.

Just like their pioneering predecessors, the 2007 All Golds included one Australian in their midst. A centenary ago, it was Dally Messenger, and at Warrington it was former Warriors hooker Steve Price. For this unique match, the team was coached by Australian Wayne Bennett.

Like the 1907 tourists, it was hoped some rugby players with league backgrounds would play, but due to the World Cup taking place at the same time, this proved unworkable.

Three Kiwis legends came out of retirement to play for the All Golds – Nigel Vagana, Ruben Wiki and Stacey Jones.

The All Golds won the match 25-18. To recreate the original tour, tries were worth three points.

The game was played alongside the three Tests against Great Britain on the tour that year which Great Britain comfortably won.

Warrington was one of the original 22 clubs that formed the Northern Rugby Football Union. Warrington is the only side that has always been in the top flight of the game, but it has traditionally been a mid-table side. Since moving to their new Haliwell Jones Stadium from Wilderspool in 2003, the side has seen increased revenues and enjoyed greater success on the pitch, finishing top of the table in 2011 and lifting the League Leaders' Shield.

Heaton Park, Manchester

St Margaret's Road Car Park, St Margaret's, Manchester, M25 2SW
www.heatonpark.org.uk

On Tuesday and Wednesday afternoons, between April and September, the public is invited to play lawn bowls for £2 and emulate the competitors from the 2002 Commonwealth Games. The bowls and the shoes will be provided.

The bowling green at Heaton Park was created especially for the Commonwealth Games. The public golf course within the Heaton Park complex was designed by J.H. Taylor – a five-times winner of the British Open.

In 2002 at the Commonwealth Games, Jo Edwards and Sharon Sims teamed up to win gold in the Women's Pairs. For Edwards, winning was something of a homecoming having been born in Wirral, Merseyside – less than an hour's drive away from Manchester.

Also on the greens, the New Zealand Women's Four won bronze as did Mike Kernaghan and Marlene Castle in the Men's and Women's singles respectively.

Houldsworth Hall, Manchester

Venue no longer exists
Approximate Address: 90 Deansgate, Manchester, M3 2QC

Right in the heart of central Manchester, Houldsworth Hall held the final of the 1952 World Snooker Championship.

At the time, there was a major dispute between many of the professional players and the sport's governing body. The dispute came to a head in 1952 as nearly all of the leading players boycotted the official event and formed their own unofficial World Championship.

The unofficial version was the Professional Matchplay Championship and this tournament continued until 1957.

The official World Championship event was the last official event held until 1969. The official 1952 tournament was held between just two men –

Australian Horace Lindrum and New Zealand's Clark McConachy. The two men battled over two weeks over 143 frames. Lindrum won by 94 frames to 49. All of the frames were played – even when the match result was known. The dead frames were watched by a crowd described as 'solemn'.

For years after the match, Lindrum toured Austarlia and South Africa claiming himself as the 'undefeated world champion'.

Today Houldsworth Hall houses church administration offices and sits above an Italian restaurant.

Isle of Man

www.iomtt.com

There are certain venues around the UK, when you can name a suburb or village and the sport immediately comes to mind. Areas that are more famous for their sport include Wimbledon, Rugby, Badminton, Aintree, Ascot and Twickenham. But, on a global scale, there are very few nations where this applies. Monaco and its Grand Prix is an example but even there, many people will think about the Casino or the glamour or the Royal family first.

But, when it comes to the Isle of Man, it is synonymous with Motorbike racing and its annual TT races.

In the Irish Sea, between Great Britain and Ireland, the Isle of Man is officially a self-governing nation. You can fly from many UK airports, but taking the ferry is part of the fun of getting there. The port of Douglas is just under three hours from Belfast or Dublin, and two and three-quarter hours from Liverpool on the Seacat. Just over 80,000 people live on the island – more than half were born away from the island and have moved there because of the low tax system.

But, for two weeks, as May turns into June, The Isle of Man becomes the home to motorbikes, petrol-heads and racing fans. The TT stands for Tourist Trophy and it takes over the Island. It is the road racing capital of the world and many fans consider it almost like a pilgrimage to visit. It is written in law that the roads can be closed.

The race dates back to 1907, and the famous Snaefell Mountain course was first used in 1911 – making it the oldest motor racing circuit still in use. Each lap is over 60 kms and goes from sea level to almost 400 metres above sea level at its highest point.

While the Queen is the country's reigning monarch as the Lord of Man, the 'king' of the TT was Joey Dunlop. The Northern Irishman had 26 wins and he ruled the roost. He completed TT hat-tricks three times. He died in 2000 in Estonia doing what he loved – riding a motorbike at high speed.

Dunlop beat New Zealander Bruce Anstey in his last ever TT race in 2000 in the Lightweight 250 race. Since that race, Anstey has gone on to win seven TT races in total for his Suzuki team (and he's been on the podium 20 times).

The first New Zealander to compete was Alex Anderson in 1914. In 1933 Sydney Moses became the first Kiwi to complete an Isle of Man TT and Charles Goldberg was the first to finish inside the top 10 in 1936.

The first New Zealander to win a race on the island was Rod Coleman in the Junior TT in 1954. Hugh Anderson won twice in 1963 and in 1964.

Aboard a Suzuki, Graeme Crosby became the first New Zealander to win

New Zealander Bruce Anstey on track aboard his Padgetts Racing machine during the 2011 Isle of Man Senior TT. (Photo courtesy of www.iomtt.com)

the Senior TT in 1980. This is the blue ribbon event of the entire fortnight. That same year he finished second in the F1 race and won that a year later.

Robert Holden won the Single Cylinder TT race in 1995, but sadly in 1996, he died on track at Glen Helen while practising. Tragically, other New Zealanders have died while competing in the Isle of Man TT – Mike Adler in 1978 and Stu Murdoch in 1999.

There is no doubting the danger – over 200 people have been killed in the race or in official practice. The roads are tight, twisting, slippery, and are often flanked by stone walls or buildings, and when the weather is bad, the danger is magnified.

Apart from watching the racing, many fans take the opportunity to ride a section of the course on what has become known as 'Mad Sunday'. This takes place on the mountain section of the course from Ramsey to Douglas. Many dress up in costume and in the past some have been dressed in 'very little'.

If you are going to the Isle of Man TT, the iconic place to sit and watch is from the Grandstand at Douglas. You will see riders race at speeds of 170 miles per hour heading towards the hill. From the grandstand you will also see the pit lane and the podium.

Elsewhere around the almost 40 miles of track, local organisations and residents lay on spectator areas including bars and toilets. Ballaugh Bridge is a great area from where to watch the action, as is the always-busy Raven pub. Some areas are prohibited for spectators, and it's worth finding this out beforehand. The street parties at night after the racing is complete are great fun and it is recommended to try the local Manx Ale.

Langtree Park

McManus Drive, St Helens, Merseyside, WA9 3AL
www.saintsrlfc.com

When New Zealanders think of English rugby league, only a handful of teams come to mind and St Helens has always been near the forefront.

The club is the second most successful team in the game behind their arch-rival Wigan. St Helens have been League champions 12 times and have also won the Challenge Cup 12 times.

St Helens first ever overseas signing was New Zealander Arthur Kelly after the 1907 All Golds tour. He played 64 games and convinced the club to sign his friend and compatriot, Hubert Turtill, who played over 130 games for the club.

Kelly and Turtill were the first of many New Zealanders to play at St Helens former stadium, Knowsley Road. Sean Hoppe, Kevin Iro, Tea Ropati, Jason Cayless and Willie Talau have all played at St Helens in the last 20 years.

Stretching back into the archives, New Zealanders who have played at St Helens have included great names in rugby league such as Archie Waddell, Roy Hardgrave and Louis Hutt.

New Zealand's Mike McClennan managed St Helens between 1990 and 1993. Former Warriors and Kiwis coach, Daniel Anderson led the team from 2005 to 2008 winning the League title and three consecutive Challenge Cups.

In 2010 Francis Meli, Tony Puletua and Sia Soliola all played for St Helens as the team said goodbye to their old Knowsley Road stadium.

It had been the team's home since 1890 but was in disrepair and belonged to a former age. It lacked the standard of facilities fans demand of a modern stadium – the paint was peeling, the stands shook and there were not even enough toilets for the fans.

Langtree Park is a state-of-the-art new stadium in the heart of St Helens town centre, and the team kicked off in 2012 with a game against Widnes. New Zealander Lance Hohaia made his debut for St Helens in this friendly match.

Maine Road, Manchester

Stadium no longer exists
Approximate Address: Blue Moon Way, Manchester, M14 7SH

This was home field to Manchester City until the club moved to their new stadium after the 2002 Commonwealth Games.

Maine Road was known as the Wembley of the North and they used to be able to cram more than 80,000 people in. Up to the end of the 2011-12 season the club has won the FA Cup five times and the League three times in total.

Historically, the team's most successful moment in time was in the late

1960s and early 70s under the managing team of Joe Mercer and Malcolm Allison. It was under their stewardship that Manchester City won the league title in 1967-68 beating cross-town rivals Manchester United into second place. They won the FA Cup in 1969 and in 1970 won the European Cup Winners' Cup.

But regardless of what league the team was in, the fans were always dedicated. Over 30,000 fans turned up each week to watch Manchester City when they were playing in the third tier of the game. The fans sing their team anthem *Blue Moon* with passion.

In 1987 a craze took off among football fans for bringing inflatable toys to the match. The craze started at Maine Road in honour of Imre 'Banana' Varadi. By 1988 the craze had spread across the country as West Ham fans took inflatable hammers to the game, Grimsby fans carried inflatable fish and Bury fans found inflatable black puddings. For a season it brought fun back to the terraces but the fad ended as quickly as it began.

Manchester City's last game at Maine Road ended in a defeat 1-0 against Southampton. Fans described it as: 'Of course, that's City being City!'

On the 1953-54 tour, The All Blacks played a North-Western Counties team and 25,000 fans went to Maine Road. The All Blacks won 17-3 that day.

Maine Road was also the host of major rugby league tournaments and between 1938 and 1956 it hosted the end of season Championship match.

Maine Road also played host to the Clash of the Codes. In 1996 an inter-code series between Bath and Wigan took place. The rugby league match was played at Maine Road. Martin Offiah scored six tries for Wigan and the Cherry and Whites won 82-6. The return match was at Twickenham. Two New Zealanders played on the winning side – Henry Paul and Va'aiga Tuigamala – both would eventually switch codes to play rugby union.

The stadium was demolished and is now the site of a housing development but there is a public art display in memory of the venue and is situated where the centre of the pitch used to be.

Manchester Central Convention Complex

(Formerly GMEX)
Petersfield, Manchester, M2 3GX
www.manchestercentral.co.uk

GMEX, which has now become part of Manchester Central Convention Complex, was one of the key venues at the Commonwealth Games in 2002.

The vaulted arches, station clock and the building's iconic gable have made it a much-loved feature of the city's skyline and an integral part of Manchester for almost 130 years. At the 2002 Commonwealth Games, Judo, Gymnastics, Weightlifting and Wrestling all took place at the venue.

For New Zealand, Nigel Avery won two gold medals and a silver medal in the 105kg+ category. His success led him to carry the flag at the closing ceremony. Olivia Baker also won a silver medal and two bronze medals while Terry Hughes won two weightlifting bronze medals.

On the judo mats, Tim Slyfield won a bronze medal in the men's 73-81kg weight range losing to eventual champion Graeme Randall from Scotland.

Manchester National Squash Centre

Sportcity, Rowsley Street, Manchester, M11 3FF
www.manchestersportandleisure.org

England Squash and Racketball has its headquarters as part of Manchester National Squash Centre at the Sportcity complex that was built for the 2002 Commonwealth Games.

At those games, only the second Commonwealth Games since Squash had been introduced, New Zealand won two gold medals on the courts.

In the Women's Doubles, Lelani Rorani (née Joyce – she got married soon before the start of the Games) made her comeback from injury and combined with Carol Owens to win the Gold medal.

In the final set, the pair came back from 10-6 down to win 15-13 in a thrilling match.

Rorani then partnered with London based Glen Wilson to win the Mixed Doubles final. Wilson was full of praise for his partner describing her as 'the shotmaker and the brilliance of the team' and himself as the 'workhorse.'

Rorani was full of praise for both her teammates claiming they were the reasons for the gold medals. This was Rorani's last squash event as she announced her retirement immediately after the Games.

Carol Owens had only recently become a New Zealand citizen, having played previously for Australia at the 1998 Commonwealth Games in Kuala Lumpur.

As well as gold with Rorani, Owens won a Silver medal in the Women's Singles losing the final to Australia's Sarah Fitzgerald.

Manchester Velodrome

Manchester, M11 4DQ
www.nationalcyclingcentre.com

This indoor track cycling venue hosted cycling events at the 2002 Commonwealth Games as well as three World Championships in 1996, 2000 and 2008. It is also the busiest Velodrome in the world.

The Velodrome is the home of the British Cycling Centre and the country's top cyclists are all based here. This world class training venue has been a major factor in Britain's recent success in cycling.

There is also an indoor BMX Centre adjoining the Velodrome. There is only one other indoor BMX Centre on this scale in the world and it makes the National Cycling Centre a multi-discipline VeloPark.

Great Britain won nine medals at the World Championships held on the track and seven gold medals in the 2008 Beijing Olympics.

Speaking soon after the 2008 Olympics Jim Battle, the deputy leader of Manchester City Council said: 'Manchester's Velodrome is the centre of excellence for our homegrown cycling talent and is the home of British cycling. Along with the other world-class facilities at Sportcity, it makes Manchester stand out on the world sporting map. Commitment to sport and regeneration turned the site of an old power station into a world beating powerhouse of sporting excellence and an Olympic medal gold mine.'

In 2008 New Zealander Hayden Godfrey won the Men's Omnium on the track as part of the World Championships.

Godfrey was replicating the success of fellow Kiwis Greg Henderson and Sarah Ulmer who both won gold medals at the Commonwealth Games, six years earlier on the same track.

In those Commonwealth Games, Greg Henderson won a gold medal in the Men's Points Race. He also won a bronze medal in the Men's Team Pursuit with Matthew Randall, Hayden Roulston and Lee Vertongen. Sarah Ulmer retained her Individual Pursuit Commonwealth title and set a new Games record in the process.

Old Trafford Cricket Ground

Old Trafford Cricket Club, Talbot Road, Manchester, M16 0PX
www.lccc.co.uk

This is the home to Lancashire County Cricket Club.

New Zealand have played seven Test matches on the ground, but have yet to win. Of the four drawn matches in 1931, 1949, 1994 and 1999, only in 1949 was the match not badly affected by the weather. New Zealand was beaten by England in 1937, 1958 and in 2008.

New Zealand has also lost two World Cup semi-final matches on the ground – in 1979 to England and in 1999 to Pakistan.

Most recently in 2008, rain played a part but not enough to save New Zealand as they were comprehensively beaten by an innings and nine runs. England made 364 and then dismissed New Zealand for 123 and 232.

New Zealanders to have played for the County side include Danny Morrison, Nathan Astle, Lou Vincent and Nathan McCullum.

Old Trafford tends to favour spin bowling and two remarkable cricketing events have taken place on the ground. In 1956 English spinner Jim Laker took 10-53 – the first man to take ten wickets in an innings and only repeated once since then. Laker also took 9-37 in the first innings giving him 19-90 for the match – which still stands as a record today.

Secondly, it was at Old Trafford, with his first ball in Ashes cricket, that Shane Warne dismissed Mike Gatting with a delivery widely described as, 'the ball of the century'. The ball was the catalyst to bring leg spin bowling back into fashion and Warne would go on to take over 700 test wickets.

One-day cricket was born at Old Trafford as in 1963 Lancashire hosted Leicestershire in the first ever first class one-day cricket match. Ironically, because of rain, the match took two days to complete!

The Lancashire team has traditionally been very strong at the one-day game, winning the one-day trophy four times during the 1990s. In 2011, the club celebrated winning the County Championship for the first time since 1950.

Old Trafford

Sir Matt Busby Way, Old Trafford, Manchester, M16 0RA
www.manutd.com

This is the footballing home to Manchester United and is one of the most awe-inspiring stadia in the UK. It is the third largest stadium in terms of capacity with over 76,000 fans cramming in to watch the Red Devils at play.

The club was founded in 1878 and changed its name to Manchester United in 1902. The club moved into Old Trafford in 1910.

Manchester United is the most successful club in English football having recently won their 19th title to go ahead of their arch rivals Liverpool. They have won the FA Cup a record 11 times and the European Cup three times.

The stadium is nicknamed the Theatre of Dreams – a name allegedly coined by legendary former player and club Ambassador Sir Bobby Charlton.

Going to the ground, you will pass Matt Busby Way. The club has endured its share of tragedy as well as triumph. Busby was the manager in 1958 at the time of the Munich air crash when eight players and a further 15 officials, journalists and supporters were killed when returning from a match in Yugoslavia. Busby himself was badly hurt in the crash.

The stadium was bombed in 1941 during World War Two and the club was forced to play across town at Maine Road until 1949.

Inside the ground, the Stretford End is the most well-known stand and is home to the most passionate supporters. Manchester United legend Denis Law was known as the King of the Stretford end.

Across the UK, no club draws greater emotion than Manchester United. You are either a fan of the club or you hate them – there seems little in between. Away fans normally point to the fact that few Manchester United fans live in Manchester. Tottenham Hotspur fans chant: 'we'll see you back in London!' while other clubs sing: 'We support our local club.'

The stadium has hosted the FA Cup final three times. In 1966 Old Trafford hosted group matches of the World Cup and at the 2012 Olympics there were quarter-final and semi-final matches.

In 2000 it was at Old Trafford where New Zealand lost to Australia in the final of the Rugby League World Cup. It is also the permanent home of the Super League Grand final.

Old Trafford is the only English stadium outside London, where the All Blacks have played a Test match against England. The All Blacks won 25-8 on the 1997 tour. That day is remembered as much for the rugby as the pre-match haka when Richard Cockerill eyeballed Norm Hewitt and the two almost came to blows. A year later England toured New Zealand and the two continued their argument in the streets of Dunedin and Cockerill was left with a blackened eye.

The All Blacks 'Invincibles' beat a Lancashire team 23-0 on the 1924-25 tour in front of 35,000 spectators.

The stadium has also staged boxing fights – in 1993 in front of 43,000 fans Nigel Benn and Chris Eubank fought a rematch of their classic 1990 fight. The two British fighters were watched worldwide by over half a billion people. The bout ended in a draw but boxing was the winner – their two fights did what boxing rarely does – it was even better than the hype.

If you are a fan of Manchester United, the Museum on site at the ground is a showpiece of memorabilia to the club, the trophies and the legendary players. More than 200,000 people visit the Museum every year. You can also emulate your heroes and learn more about the ground by doing a guided tour.

Reebok Stadium, Bolton

Burnden Way, Bolton, BL6 6JW
www.reebok-stadium.co.uk and www.bwfc.co.uk

The Reebok Stadium was built in 1997 as the new home for Bolton Wanderers football club. In the first year in their new home, Bolton were relegated. They bounced back to the top flight within three years and spent ten years in the top flight before being relegated in 2012.

The team is known as The Trotters and have won the FA Cup four times. Nat Lofthouse scored two goals when the team last won the trophy in 1958 and the East Stand at the Reebok Stadium is named in his honour.

As with many newly built stadia, the Reebok is not in the centre of town, but in the suburbs. A recent trend has been to build a hotel into the venue and from some of these rooms, you can see onto the pitch.

The architecture of the stadium is stunning – visually dramatic and considered among the best designed new stadia since the 1990 Taylor Report, which required all major British football stadia to be fully seated.

There is a memorial at the Reebok Stadium to the 33 people who died at Bolton's previous home ground of Burnden Park. They were crushed at an FA Cup quarter-final in 1946. It is estimated 85,000 fans were packed into a stadium with a capacity of 60,000.

In the following months, the Moelwyn Hughes report, recommended that limits be placed on crowd sizes.

New Zealand played their 2000 Rugby League World Cup semi-final against England at the Reebok Stadium. At the time, this was England's biggest ever loss as the Kiwis romped to a 49-6 win. It was 6-0 after three minutes and it just got better and better for New Zealand as they scored eight tries in total to advance to the final.

New Zealand also beat Great Britain 36-16 on the ground in 1998 as part of the Test series that year.

Royal Birkdale Golf Club

Waterloo Road, Southport, PR8 2LX
www.royalbirkdale.com

Based at the heart of England's Golf Coast, this seaside links course near the resort town of Southport has been host to the Open nine times – firstly in 1954 and most recently in 2008.

More New Zealanders have played at Royal Birkdale than any other British Open venue.

In that first Open at Birkdale, New Zealand amateur Ron Timms qualified, but missed the cut by one shot with opening rounds of 80 and 72.

Ross Newdick made the cut in his second and final Open appearance on the Southport links in 1965 and eventually finished in a tie for 46th place.

Bob Charles missed the cut twice at Birkdale but in 1971, he finished 18th. That same year John Lister was 25th, Walter Godfrey was 40th, whilst Alistair Palmer and Alan Snape both missed the cut.

Five years later, in 1976, Bob Charles and Simon Owen both missed the cut and in 1983, no New Zealanders played at Birkdale – the first time no New Zealander had competed at an Open since the 1950s.

Five New Zealanders played when the Open returned to Birkdale in 1998. As well as Turner and Nobilo, Michael Long, Steve Alker and Michael Campbell all played. Turner was the best placed Kiwi in 15th behind winner Mark O'Meara.

Ten years later, the Open returned to Birkdale. Michael Campbell and David Smail both finished down the field as Ireland's Padraig Harrington retained the trophy.

Our Australian cousins have always fared well on the Birkdale links. Peter Thomson won twice here (in 1954 and 1965), Ian Baker Finch won in 1998 beating compatriot Mike Harwood. In 2008, Greg Norman turned back the years and led by two shots after three rounds but struggled on the final day to a 77 and finished third.

The club has twice hosted the Ryder Cup. In 1965, the USA won and four years later, the match finished in a 16 all tie when Jack Nicklaus famously conceded a putt on the last hole of the last match to Tony Jacklin in one of the game's greatest acts of sportsmanship.

The course has also hosted the Women's British Open five times. New Zealand's Lynette Brooky competed at Royal Birkdale in 2000, 2005 and 2010 but missed the cut in all three events.

On a still day at Birkdale, the bunkers and undulating greens provide the golf course's defence, but when the wind blows straight off the Irish Sea, you will need to play your very best to just survive.

Royal Lytham & St Annes Golf Club

Links Gate, Lytham St Annes, Lancashire, FY8 3LQ
www.royallytham.org

It is not beautiful in the traditional sense of the golfing links word. It is set in an area of housing, beside a busy railway line. It is not set beside the beach, but is more than half a mile from the Fylde coast.

The wind often blows hard across the course and you will spend a lot of time playing out of bunkers as there are over 200 on the course.

But the more time you spend there, the more the course envelops you, the more you feel its traditions and its history the more beautiful you will begin to find this wonderful links course.

The plaque on the 17th hole at Royal Lytham & St Annes Golf Club celebrating esteemed American amateur golfer Bobby Jones.

In 2012 Royal Lytham & St Annes hosted the British Open for the 11th time.

The famed American amateur Bobby Jones won here when the Open was first staged here in 1926. He had won the US Open at Inwood Country Club, New York a month earlier and he became the first man to complete that double. Famously, he left the course between the two rounds and forgot his competitor badge. A security guard did not recognise him, so Jones calmly went to the desk and paid as a spectator to get back on to the course.

You can see the plaque on the 17th hole from where Jones played a remarkable second shot in the final round. The Mashie he used to play this shot is kept on display in the clubhouse along with a wide collection of other historic mementos.

Other British Open winners have included Peter Thomson, Gary Player and the late Seve Ballesteros who won at Royal Lytham twice. American Tom Lehman was victorious and in 2001 David Duval claimed his only major title.

But for New Zealand sports fans, Royal Lytham & St Annes Golf Club will always be associated with only one name – Sir Robert James Charles.

In 1963, on the back of victory at the Houston Classic, Charles came to Royal Lytham. In fact Charles was returning to Lytham, as he played there in 1958 as a 22-year-old amateur. But in 1963, he shot 277 (-3) to tie with American Phil Rodgers. Charles won the Monday play-off over 36 holes by 8 shots. He became the first left-hander to win a major – a feat not matched until Mike Weir won The Masters in 2003.

He almost repeated the victory when the Open returned to Lytham in 1969. He led after two rounds but a third round 75 hurt his chances and he eventually finished second behind Tony Jacklin.

Thirty years after his Open victory, Charles returned to Royal Lytham and won the 1993 Senior British Open. He played his last ever Open at Royal Lytham in 2001.

If you have the opportunity to go and play Royal Lytham, stay overnight at the Dormy House which overlooks the course and you can wake up and look out over the first tee as you get ready for the day ahead.

Royal Lytham & St Annes also hosted the Ryder Cup in 1961 and 1971 and it has hosted the Women's Open four times – most recently in 2009 when Catriona Matthew claimed the victory.

Table Tennis Centre

Venue no longer exists

Whiff-Whaff, Flim-Flam, Gossima as well as Ping-Pong are some of the names the sport of Table Tennis has been previously been known.

When the International Federation was formed in 1926, they chose Table Tennis because the games manufacturer Parker Bros had already patented the name Ping Pong.

In 2002, Table Tennis made its debut at the Commonwealth Games in Manchester. Men's and Women's Singles and Doubles were played as well as Mixed Doubles and a Teams' event.

New Zealand's Chunli Li won medals in all four of the events she entered. She won gold in the Singles, a silver medal with Karen Li in the Women's doubles and bronze medals with Peter Jackson in the mixed doubles as well as the Teams' event. In doing so, she became the first New Zealander to ever win four medals at one Commonwealth Games.

At the conclusion of the Games, the Table Tennis centre made way for the Tennis centre as part of the Sport City complex which also includes the Etihad Stadium as well as the National Squash Centre and the Manchester Velodrome. The tennis centre has six indoor courts and six outdoor courts and can be booked by members of the general public.

Yorkshire and the North East

Both of these areas have interesting and varied sporting histories and are steeped in tradition and success.

Football dominates the North East and the Tyne-Wear derby between Newcastle and Sunderland is fiercely contested.

Durham is a beautiful university city and its cathedral is awe-inspiring.

Visiting Yorkshire is always special. There is a rugged beauty on the moors and the stone buildings across the country offer a feeling of solidity and something you can trust.

The working background of the county comes through in the games people play. Alongside Lancashire, the area is a rugby league hotbed with teams like Hull, Leeds and Bradford. The game was born in a Huddersfield hotel and developed here.

Football is passionately supported but teams from Yorkshire have not fared well recently. No team from Yorkshire has been in the Premier League since Leeds in 2004. The history of football runs deep as Sheffield FC is recognised as the oldest club in the world.

Sheffield is the nation's snooker capital. The Crucible in the city centre is under the spotlight for the two weeks of the World Championship but the National academy is also based here.

Cricket in Yorkshire is popular and Headingley is a great venue to watch cricket on a sunny day.

The area has never had a strong rugby union base – its working-class roots have much to do with this.

Yorkshire is a special area to visit for New Zealanders. Get out and explore the moors, shop in Leeds, visit the elegant towns of Harrogate and York or delve into Great Britain's industrial past in towns like Bradford and Barnsley. Visit Bronte country where the leading literary sisters wrote classics such as Jane Eyre and Wuthering Heights.

What's more you can visit the village of Marton where Captain Cook was born or visit his Memorial Museum in Whitby.

Barley Mow, Bramley

The Barley Mow Pub, Bramley, Lower Town Street, Bramley, Leeds,
LS13 3EN
www.sizzlingpubs.co.uk

Bramley has become a suburb of Leeds, gobbled up as the city has grown in size.

Barley Mow was home to local rugby league team, Bramley – and it was on this ground that the 'All Golds' (as they were later to become known) touring side of 1907 played their first game.

The 1907 All Golds tour played a large part in the development of rugby league in the UK – but even more so in New Zealand and Australia.

The tour was set against a backdrop of frustration over money by the players. The 1905 tour by The Originals made a huge profit for the New Zealand Rugby Union but the players were only paid their expenses. Because the 1905 tour only briefly visited Yorkshire, the Northern Union teams were very enthusiastic to host a team from the Antipodes and play them under Northern Union rules.

The 1907 tour was devised and led by Albert Henry Baskerville and ably assisted by George William Smith. The Baskerville Shield, the trophy for Test series between UK and NZ, is named in his honour. One of the selectors was Duncan McGregor who had scored four tries for the All Blacks in their 15-0 win against England at Crystal Palace in 1905.

Amazingly by today's standards, players had to apply to go on the tour because it would cost them an investment of £50 each and then any subsequent profits would be shared.

The team was primarily made up of New Zealanders but Dally Messenger joined the team as captain after the first three games in Sydney. The team was made up of rugby players including William Mackrell who was on the 1905 Originals tour and many leading provincial players.

After a long trip, the team arrived at Leeds train station to be greeted by 6,000 people. Over the next fortnight, they acclimatised to the colder weather and learnt the Northern Union rules they would be playing.

On 9 October 1907 at Barley Mow, the Professional All Blacks won 25 – 6. 'All Golds' was a term to be used later. The team went on to win 19 of their 35 matches in the UK.

While the players did not view themselves as professionals, the New Zealand Rugby Union did, and every player received life bans. Many of the players subsequently returned to the UK to take up contracts with Northern Union teams.

In 2007 the centenary was celebrated as the All Golds toured the UK and played three Tests and a match against a Northern Union selection. Australian Steve Price reprised the role of Dally Messenger and captained the team.

Barley Mow has now been transformed into a housing estate but a blue plaque at the Sizzling Barley Mow Pub commemorates the tour and the first ever international rugby league tour match. The pub was chosen as it acted as headquarters for the Bramley rugby league club and it was the changing rooms for the 1907 All Golds team. Have a drink in the pub and raise a glass to the All Golds.

Burghley

Burghley House, Stamford, Lincolnshire, PE9 3JY
www.burghley-horse.co.uk and www.burghley.co.uk

Set in the shadows of an imposing grand stately home, The Land Rover Burghley Horse Trials is one of the major events on the worldwide Three Day Eventing calendar.

Burghley House is a grand 16th-century country house and one of the great remaining examples of Elizabethan architecture. Interestingly, the house was built in the shape of the letter E to honour Queen Elizabeth I.

The house is open to the public from spring through until autumn and gives a fascinating insight into a time gone by.

But in August-September it is Burghley's parkland, designed by Capability Brown, that is of most interest to sports fans – Burghley is one of only six equestrian venues worldwide to provide CCI**** (Concours Compleat International) competition.

Between 1987 and 2001 New Zealanders claimed the title nine out of 15 times. Mark Todd won five times and both Andrew Nicholson and Blyth Tait each won twice.

In 1987 Todd claimed first and second aboard different horses and Blyth Tait was the second person to do it in 1998. In 2001 three New Zealanders were on the Podium. Tait won from Nicholson and Dan Jocelyn was third.

More recently, Caroline Powell rode Lenamore to victory in 2010, claiming the £50,000 first prize as did Nicholson abroad in 2012.

In previous years, Her Royal Highness Princess Anne won in 1971 aboard Doublet while her daughter Zara finished second in 2003.

Burghley is a very social occasion for spectators. Picnics and a glass or two of something is a wonderful way to say goodbye to the summer. In 2011 2,000 bottles of Champagne were sold and 7,000 glasses of Pimms.

New Zealand's Caroline Powell celebrates winning the Land Rover
Burghley Horse Trials in 2010. (Picture: Kit Houghton)

New Zealand's Andrew Nicholson in action at The Land Rover
Burghley Horse Trials. (Picture: Kit Houghton)

Coral Windows Stadium

Valley Parade, Bradford,BD8 7DY
www.bradfordcityfc.co.uk

The football club Bradford City, play their home matches on this ground – previously known as Valley Parade. Known as The Bantams, the team has only twice graced the top flight of the game in the last 90 years.

In 1999-2000 Bradford finished one place above the relegation zone in 17th with a surprise final day victory over Liverpool. A season later the team finished 16 points from safety in last position – winning only five of their 38 games.

Valley Parade started as the home ground for Northern Union (rugby league) team, Manningham. The team were the first winners of the League Championship in 1896 but they switched to football in 1903.

The present FA Cup was made by Fattorini's of Bradford and by coincidence Bradford City were the first team to win it in 1911. This is the only time Bradford have won the FA Cup.

New Zealand's 2010 World Cup goalkeeper Mark Paston played 14 times for Bradford City during the 2003-04 season as the Bantams were relegated.

The away fans are seated to the side of the pitch whereas in most grounds the away fans sit behind the goal.

Tragedy struck Valley Parade in May 1985 when a fire broke out in a stand during a match between Bradford and Lincoln City. The day was meant to be one of celebration as the club lifted the Third Division League trophy but instead 56 people died and many others were injured.

It is believed the fateful fire started when a cigarette or match was dropped through a seat onto a pile of rubbish. Fans escaped as best they could – onto the pitch or through turnstiles but the wooden roof caught fire and within four minutes the entire stand was engulfed in flames.

As a result of that tragic afternoon, the consequent Popplewell Inquiry prohibited the construction of new wooden grandstands at all UK sports grounds.

There are two memorials at the ground to remember that awful May afternoon and there is another memorial in the centre of Bradford outside the Town Hall.

The Bradford disaster appeal raised more than £3.5 million. One such event was a recreation of the 1966 World Cup final – with the original England and West German players involved.

Of the 56 casualties, two were Lincoln City fans. When Lincoln renovated their home ground in 1990, the Stacey-West stand was named in honour of those two fans.

Elland Road

Elland Road, Leeds, LS11 0SE
www.leedsunited.com

This stadium has been the footballing home of Leeds United for almost 100 years.

The team peaked in the 1960s and 70s under manager Don Revie as the club won two League titles, the FA Cup and the League Cup.

The club returned to the good old days in the 1990s, including winning the League in 1991-92. By the end of the millennium, Leeds was riding the crest of a wave, playing in European competitions and had an all-star team.

But Leeds' financial bubble burst and over the next few years the club spiralled downwards both on and off the pitch. The club nearly went bankrupt and spent three seasons playing in the third tier of English football.

But throughout it all, Leeds fans have always stuck with their team.

Many large English cities have two or three teams but Leeds is the only club in town. Elland Road is an intense and vociferous stadium – even in the bad years 25,000 people were going to each game. Sir Alex Ferguson, manager of bitter rival Manchester United, called the ground 'the most intimidating venue in Europe'.

Like New Zealand's football team, Leeds play in an all white strip. Danny Hay from Auckland played for the club between 1999 and 2001. He played against Liverpool, Manchester United, Tottenham and Bradford in the League and was part of the team beaten 4-0 by Barcelona in the Champions League.

Elland Road has also been a rugby league venue, most famously when the Kiwis beat Australia 24-0 in the final of the 2005 Tri-Nations. It hosted the final of the Four Nations in 2011 when Australia beat England by 30-8.

John Smith Stadium, Huddersfield

(Previously known as Alfred McAlpine Stadium and Galpharm Stadium)
Stadium Way, Huddersfield, HD1 6PG
www.johnsmithstadium.com

New Zealand rugby supporters warmly remember this stadium as it hosted New Zealand's group game against Italy in the 1999 Rugby World Cup.

New Zealand won by 101 – 3. That day 10 different All Blacks scored including Jeff Wilson who bagged a hat-trick and overtook John Kirwan to become the country's highest try scorer.

On the ground, New Zealand lost to Australia in the semi-final of the 1995 Rugby League World Cup. While the Kangaroos were weakened by the NRL versus Super League war, the Australians won 30 – 20 in extra-time and went on to beat England in the final.

The Stadium was built in 1994 and is the home for Huddersfield Town football club and rugby league's Huddersfield Giants.

Before the construction of this stadium, Huddersfield Town played at Leeds Road. The team shares a record with Arsenal, Liverpool and Manchester United. These four are the only teams to have ever won three successive League titles – Huddersfield's Terriers did it from 1923-24 through to the 1925-26 seasons.

As well as beating Italy in the World Cup, the All Blacks also played here on the 1997 tour against an Emerging England XV. New Zealand won 59 – 22 on that day.

Conrad Byrne, William Trevarthen and Edgar Wrigley all toured with the All Golds in 1907-08 and then signed for Huddersfield.

In the 1950s, former All Black Peter 'Sammy' Henderson signed to play rugby league for Huddersfield and played for the club for seven years scoring over 200 tries in more than 250 games and helping them win the Challenge Cup in 1953. Henderson is renowned as one of the fastest All Black wingers ever as indicated by the bronze medal he won as a sprinter at the 1950 Empire Games in Auckland.

More recently, Robbie Paul played 52 games for Huddersfield and David Faiumu moved to the club in 2009 and David Fa'alogo in 2010.

Headingley Carnegie Cricket Ground

Address: St Michael's Lane, Leeds, LS6 3BU
www.yorkshireccc.com

On the 10th New Zealand cricket tour, after 52 years and at the 29th attempt, New Zealand beat England in a Test cricket match on English soil.

At the end of July 1983, Lance Cairns was New Zealand's bowling hero on the first day as he took seven wickets. Bruce Edgar, John Wright and Richard Hadlee all made runs as New Zealand made 377. Ewan Chatfield then took five wickets in a Test for the first time as England could only make 252.

New Zealand needed 101 to win. The nerves jangled but on 31 July, Jeremy Coney hit the winning runs and for this Headingley will live long in the memories of New Zealand cricket fans. The team lost the other three Tests on this tour but the duck was broken and that first series victory would come three years later.

When New Zealand returned to Headingley on the 2004 tour the team was blighted by injuries – they had to resort to calling on Aucklander Rob Nicol as a third substitute fielder who was watching from the stands. New Zealand coach at the time John Bracewell said: 'We found Rob on the terraces – luckily before he went to the bar.'

New Zealand also played India in the 1979 World Cup at the ground and won that group game by restricting India to 182 from their 60 overs.

Headingley was also the venue for arguably test cricket's most memorable comeback. In 1981, England was 135-7 in their second innings, still almost 100 runs in arrears of Australia having been made to follow on. Bookmakers at the ground quoted England at 500-1 to win.

Ian Botham had other ideas as he strode to the pitch and in swashbuckling style scored his century off just 87 balls and eventually finished on 149. A total of 356 gave England hope.

Chasing a meagre 130 for victory, Australia were still the favourites – even more so when they reached 56-1. But England's Bob Willis was in devastating form with the ball and took 8-43, Australia was dismissed for 111 and the fairytale comeback was complete.

The ground has been the home of Yorkshire County since 1891 and they are the most successful county side with 34 County Championships (two of them shared).

Headingley Carnegie Stadium

St Michael's Lane, Leeds, LS6 3BR
www.leedsrugby.com

At Headingly there are two separate pitches, one for Rugby and one for Cricket. They are linked in the middle by a two-sided stand for spectators which faces both grounds.

New Zealand has played both rugby league tests and rugby union matches on the ground. It is where the famous 1907 All Golds played their first test against England, but lost 14-6.

Headingley was used for the first ever Challenge Cup final. In April 1897, Batley beat St Helens by 10-3 in front of a crowd of almost 14,000. The photograph from that match is amazing as the St Helens team are unrecognisable as a team because none of them are wearing the same jersey.

The Kiwis have played Rugby League World Cup matches at Headingley. In the 1985-88 version, New Zealand drew with England. In the 1960 World Cup match, the Kiwis lost 21-15 to Australia but the match is well remembered for a try by New Zealand legend, George Menzies.

In 2011 and 2012, akin to State of Origin, a match between England and The Exiles was played at Headingley. The Exiles were chosen from New Zealanders and Australians who ply their trade in the UK.

Numerous New Zealanders have played for the rugby league side Leeds (now Leeds Rhinos) who call Headingley home. Harold Rowe and Joseph Lavery were two of the first signings who played for the All Golds in 1907 and went on to sign for Leeds after the tour finished.

Leeds signed John Gallagher to play rugby league in 1989 after 18 Tests for the All Blacks including the 1987 World Cup victory over France. Gallagher's switch was generally viewed as unsuccessful and he eventually returned to playing rugby. Craig Innes followed Gallagher to Leeds after the 1991 World Cup and went on to a very successful career in the sport – becoming a dual sport international when he played for The Rest of the World in a Test match against Australia.

Richie Blackmore, Kevin Iro, Willie Poching, Kylie Leuluai, Clinton Toopi and Brent Webb are among the Kiwis to have all played in the blue and yellow of Leeds in the Super League era. Ali Lauititi is Leeds' most successful overseas signing. He has played in five winning Super League finals including 2011 when Leeds beat St Helens.

On a rugby front, the All Blacks have only played once on the ground – the Originals beat Yorkshire by 40-0 in December 1905.

Leeds Carnegie currently play their rugby in the second division Championship. Stephen Bachop and Justin Marshall have both played for Leeds in the past.

KC Stadium

KC Stadium, Walton Street, Hull, HU3 6HU
www.hullfc.com and www.hulltigers.com

The KC Stadium is a council owned stadium and home to Hull City's football team and the rugby league club Hull FC.

The rugby league team moved from their previous ground, The Boulevard and Hull City previously played at Boothferry Park. The teams played their first competitive games at the new ground in 2003.

In rugby league, the Kiwis have twice played at the stadium. In 2004, Great Britain beat New Zealand 26-24. In the 2011 Four Nations rugby league tournament New Zealand lost to England, by the score of 28-6 in front of more than 25,000 fans at the KC Stadium.

The KC Stadium will host games during the 2013 Rugby League World Cup.

Hull FC Rugby was one of the founding teams of Northern Union – so is one of the 22 world's rugby league clubs in the world.

Hull has won the Challenge Cup only once – when they beat Leeds in the final in 2005 at the Millennium Stadium, Cardiff. Three New Zealanders played that day for Hull – Richard Swain and Stephen Kearney as well as Motu Tony who scored the first try.

Other New Zealanders to have played for Hull FC (since the move to the KC) have included Richie Barnett, Sione Faumuina and Aaron Heremaia.

Before moving to the KC Stadium, Hull City was playing in the fourth tier of English football. Within five years, they had reached the Premier League. The club was in the top flight for two years but were relegated back to the Championship in May 2010.

The Wellington Inn is a good place for a drink before or after the match whether you're watching football or rugby league.

North Marine Road Cricket Ground

North Marine Road, Scarborough, YO12 7TJ
www.scarboroughcricket.co.uk

In what has often been the last match of a cricket tour to the UK, New Zealand teams have played eight times as part of the Scarborough cricket festival.

This annual match is organised by the Yorkshire County Cricket Club and watched at North Marine Road in the early September sunshine by crowds of holidaymakers.

Numerous touring sides have played as part of the festival but a common match in the earliest days was between 'The Players' and 'The Gentlemen' (a 156 year rivalry first played in 1806).

It was here a New Zealand Services team played a team led by HDG Leveson-Gower in 1945. This was the only first class match played on this tour. For New Zealand, Martin Donnelly (named as one of the five Wisden cricketers of the year) scored 100 and 86 and New Zealand declared their second innings thinking the match was safe but the hosts scored 63 runs in 25 minutes to steal the victory.

North Marine Road has small boundaries and a hard outfield so run scoring has normally been prolific at Yorkshire's sunniest coastal resort. Ken Rutherford smashed 317 when New Zealand toured in 1986.

It was also here that New Zealand Women scored their highest ever Test total in 1996 when they made 517 against England. Kirsty Flavell became the first woman to score a Test double century, scoring 204.

After the cricket is finished for the day, fans and other casual acquaintances of the game, return to their beach chairs and look out over the cold North Sea. Fish and chips for dinner and as the sun sets, the Northern Hemisphere begins to brace itself for the cold months ahead.

Probiz Coliseum

The PROBIZ Coliseum, Wheldon Road, Castleford, WF10 2SD
www.castigers.com

Home to rugby league team Castleford, this stadium was previously named The Jungle.

Built in 1927, today the ground is dilapidated and plans are in motion for a new stadium to be ready during 2013.

At The Jungle, in the 2000 Rugby League World Cup quarter-final, New Zealand beat France 54-6 as Robbie Paul scored a hat-trick of tries.

Tawerau Nikau, Brendon Tuuta, Frano Botica, Awen Guttenbeil, Gary Freeman, Richie Blackmore and Tony Kemp among others have all played for

Pitch-side entertainment at the Probiz Coliseum.

Castleford. Many players have spoken of their love for the ground because of how close the fans are.

Castleford have won the Challenge Cup four times – most recently in 1986 but have never won the Super League or League Championship title.

The Boulevard

Stadium no longer exists
Approximate Address: Massey Close, Hull, HU3 3QT

This stadium was home to Hull FC - one of the two Rugby League teams in the city - until 2003 when the team moved to the newly constructed KC Stadium.

The Kiwis played a 1970 Rugby League World Cup match at the ground beating France 16-15 in a mud bath. This was New Zealand's only victory in the tournament that year.

In 2002 Hull played the touring Kiwis in their last ever game at The Boulevard. Under Coach Gary Freeman, the tourists trailed at half-time but came back to win.

In the early to mid 1980s four New Zealanders were playing at Hull together – Fred Ah Kuoi, future Kiwis coach Gary Kemble, James Leuluai and Dane O'Hara. This was a golden period for the club including winning the Challenge Cup in 1981-82 and the championship a season later.

Former Kiwis coach Tony 'Tank' Gordon also coached Hull in the mid 1990s.

In the late 1970s and 1980s two New Zealand Speedway racers were part of the Hull Vikings team who raced at The Boulevard. Barry Briggs raced for the Hull team in 1976 and Ivan Mauger raced for the team from 1978 through until 1981.

The Crucible

The Crucible Theatre, 55 Norfolk Street, Sheffield, S1 1DA
www.sheffieldtheatres.co.uk and www.worldsnooker.com

The theatre in central Sheffield stages shows, plays, musicals, comedians and in April and May each year it hosts the World Snooker Championship.

The Crucible has been the home to snooker's biggest event since 1977. It is an incredibly intimate location to watch snooker as the theatre seats fewer than 1,000 people.

For the first week of the tournament, there are two tables with a screen splitting the theatre in half but for the final stages of the tournament, there is only one table. Wherever your seat, you will be fewer than 20 metres from the tables and the atmosphere can be electric.

During the two weeks of the World Championships, the city of Sheffield goes Snooker loopy. There are exhibitions, special events, evenings with former stars of the game, and tables around the city.

In snooker's modern era, five names stand apart from the crowd. Stephen Hendry from Scotland has seven world championships, while England's Steve Davis and Wales' Ray Reardon both have six. John Higgins from Scotland has four world titles.

Since the millennium, one name has regularly lit up the snooker world – Ronnie O'Sullivan. He has four world championships and is the only man to have scored three maximum 147 breaks at The Crucible. His first was in 1997 – in a record five minutes and 20 seconds.

The only New Zealander to have played at The Crucible is Christchurch born Dene O'Kane who competed six times in the 80s and 90s.

O'Kane's best result was reaching the quarter-finals where he lost to Jimmy White in 1987 and to Hendry in 1992. O'Kane last competed in 1996 when he lost in the first round to Peter Ebdon who went on to make the final that year.

The George Hotel, Central Huddersfield

The George Hotel, St George's Square, Huddersfield, HD1 1JA
www.brook-hotels.co.uk and www.rlheritage.co.uk

The game of rugby league was born on 29 August 1895. It was on that date in the George Hotel in Huddersfield that the Northern Clubs of the Rugby Football Union (RFU) voted to break away from the RFU and form the Northern Rugby Football Union.

Players in the north of England traditionally came from working class backgrounds while those in the south often (but not always) came from more privileged backgrounds.

The 1895 meeting was called in response to the 1893 decision by the RFU not to make 'broken time payments' to players to make up for lost wages.

A new league was formed – this was the creation of rugby league.

All 22 teams in the first season came from Yorkshire, Lancashire or Cheshire. A ceiling was placed on the fee a player could earn and the player still had to be in full-time employment but the wheels for the professional game were in motion.

In the first two years after the breakaway the rules remained the same, but starting with the elimination of line-outs, the game of rugby league as we know it today began to take shape.

The Challenge Cup was created in 1897 (Batley beat St Helens 10–3), professionalism in 1898, a Super League of the top teams was devised for the 1901/02 season but the biggest changes were still to come.

Almost since that 1895 meeting, there had been a growing call to reduce the number of players on the field. It was argued this would introduce a more flowing and open game – which is what the paying spectators wanted. Warrington proposed dropping two players and it was agreed in 1906. Rugby League was 13-a-side.

In this same off-season the play-the-ball was created in order to eliminate fighting and the chaos within tackles.

The Northern Rugby Football Union officially changed its name to Rugby Football League in 1922.

Memorabilia about that meeting in 1895 can still be viewed throughout the George Hotel today and there is a rugby league Heritage centre in the basement of the hotel. Within this is the British Rugby League Hall of Fame.

The Great North Run

Newcastle to South Shields
www.greatrun.org

In the 1970s Brendan Foster was a leading long distance runner who ran in the Round the Bays fun run in Auckland, New Zealand.

Foster was inspired by the 50,000 fun runners who were up against leading athletes, were raising money for charity, were keeping fit and were most of all enjoying it.

The Olympic medallist was so inspired he wished to recreate the run in his native north-east England over a half marathon distance.

The first Great North Run took place in 1981 when 12,500 runners ran from Newcastle to South Shields – across the Tyne Bridge.

Today, 50,000 runners tread the same path and it is now one of the biggest running events in the world.

The Great North Run's success meant the brand expanded to include The Great Manchester Run, the Great North Mile, Great South Run, Great Australian Run and Great Ethiopian Run.

Scotland

A trip to Scotland always feels a little bit special. It's a longer trip, there's a noticeable change in the weather and the accent is markedly different. There are moments of isolation, it can feel desolate but there is raw beauty in nature – the lochs are dramatic, the views spectacular.

New Zealanders will think of Dunedin in highland tones and as they travel Scotland it is easy to see what inspired those earliest immigrants.

The contrast between Scotland's two main cities Edinburgh and Glasgow is stark.

Linked by the M8 motorway, Edinburgh has the feel of a modern cosmo-politan city – with trendy people sipping lattes who work in financial services. The city has a nod to history as the castle dominates but planning for the world of tomorrow is just as important.

At the other end of the M8 Glasgow is less refined. Glaswegians may have a pint in their hand and swearing is part of their vocabulary. When they laugh it comes from the belly and their actions speak louder than words.

The two leading football clubs have traditionally been in Glasgow – Rangers and Celtic – while the country's rugby headquarters is at Murrayfield in Edinburgh.

Glasgow will be in the spotlight in 2014 when the city hosts the Commonwealth Games. The west coast golf courses close to Glasgow (such as Troon and Prestwick) have a raw and more open feeling while Muirfield near Edinburgh is a private, exclusive refined style of links golf course.

The most famous golf course of all is St Andrews – a public course and with an ounce of luck you can get a round there.

For a price, you can stay and play at Gleneagles and Turnberry and follow in the footsteps of legends.

Away from the towns and cities, Scotland is at its best. In summer, the sunshine late into the evening creates a dramatic effect. Visit the glens, the Highlands, the islands, or the rocky coastlines.

Aberdeen Exhibition & Conference Centre

Bridge of Don, Aberdeen, AB23 8BL
www.aecc.co.uk

The landmark building in Aberdeen often hosts international conferences such as Offshore Europe, Music Concerts and Wedding Fayres but in 1999 it was the home of the British Squash Open.

New Zealand's Leilani Joyce entered the tournament as World Number three but on Saturday 11 December she beat the top seed and reigning world champion, England's Cassie Campion.

On her way to the title, Joyce beat Natalie Grinham, Sue Wright, Stephanie Brind and Natalie Grainger.

She was inspired to win the final by reading a British magazine that stated that Campion would go unbeaten for five years.

The 25-year-old from Hamilton proved them wrong winning the fourth set 10-8 to claim the title.

On the men's side that year, Canada's Jonathon Power beat Scotland's Peter Nicol when the home favourite had to retire in the third set with an upset stomach.

Other sporting events the centre has hosted include professional darts, Aberdeen Cup tennis and championship boxing fights.

Barry Buddon – Angus, Sotland

Carnoustie, Angus, DD7 7RY

The Rifle Range, next to the famed Carnoustie golf course, was the home of shooting during the 1986 Commonwealth Games in Edinburgh.

Its famed neighbour, Carnoustie Golf Course, has been an Open venue seven times up to 2007 – most famously in 1999 when Jean van de Velde threw away the title by taking a triple bogey seven on the last hole when a double bogey six would have won him the title. He lost in the Play-off to Scotland's Paul Lawrie.

As a rifle range, it was a place for regular celebration for New Zealand shooters in 1986. Greg Yelavich won two gold medals in the Free Pistol and the Air Pistol. He then teamed up with Barrie Wickens to win a bronze in the Men's Air Pistol Pairs.

The three medals Yelavich won at these games were the first of what would turn into a record haul of 13 Commonwealth medals – more than any other New Zealander.

Also in 1986, Rex Hamilton and Barry O'Neale won bronze medals – in the Pistol Pairs. John Farrell and John Woolley won bronze medals in the Men's Skeet Shooting Pairs.

Barry Buddon will again be the host of the shooting events when the Commonwealth Games return to Scotland in 2014.

The Ranges and Danger Areas are closed to the public during periods of live firing. When firing is not taking place the public can access the training area's metalled roads on foot, horseback and bicycle. You can also walk along the beaches when the flags are down and red lights extinguished. Further access to the area is not possible because of an unexploded ordnance risk.

Celtic Park

18 Kerrydale Street, Glasgow, G40 3RE
www.celticfc.net

Celtic Park is the UK's fifth largest stadium in terms of seating capacity and second in Scotland behind Murrayfield. In 2014 it will be the venue for the opening ceremony of the Commonwealth Games.

The stadium is home to Celtic Football Club – one of the two main clubs in Glasgow with the other being Rangers who play at Ibrox.

The two clubs together are known as the 'old firm' and derby matches between them are among the most intense and fiercely contested in British sport.

The rivalry follows religious lines, as Celtic supporters are traditionally Catholic while Rangers are often Protestants. Because of the strong Irish connection, the rivalry is political over the separation of Northern Ireland.

One of the wonders of sport is that it often acts as a bridge between religion, politics and race. Boxer Muhammed Ali inspired many with his stance on Vietnam, Jackie Robinson was the first black baseball player and Jesse Owens won gold medals in front of Adolf Hitler at the Berlin Olympics in 1936. But, on rare occasions sport acts as a lightning rod and sparks conflicts. The apartheid tour of the 1980s in New Zealand divided a nation and the Munich Massacre at the 1972 Olympics was a tragic moment in sporting history.

On the football field, Celtic is most famous as the first club from the UK to win the European Cup. The 'bhoys' beat Inter Milan 2-1 and became known as the 'Lisbon Lions' because the final was played in the Portuguese capital.

Celtic have been Scottish League champions 43 times while their bitter cross-town rivals Rangers have won the title 53 times. Scottish football is completely dominated by the two Glasgow sides.

Since 1893-94, Hibs, Hearts and Aberdeen have each won the title four times. 1984-85 was the last time the title was won by a team outside Glasgow – when Aberdeen was managed by Sir Alex Ferguson.

While playing for Celtic, Chris Killen became the second New Zealander, after Danny Hay, to play Champions League football when he came on as a substitute against AC Milan in October 2007.

Killen joined Celtic from Hibernian and played over 30 games for Celtic before leaving to join Middlesbrough in January 2010.

Easedale Island

by Oban, Argyll, PA34 4TB
www.stoneskimming.com

The smallest permanently inhabited island of the Inner Hebrides on Scotland's west coast is home to the World Stone Skimming Championships.

The island was formerly at the heart of the Slate mining industry and one of the disused quarries forms the setting for this quirky event.

Held at the end of September, competitors must skim a stone as far as possible.

There are rules for the event: The stone itself must be no more than three inches in diameter and it must be formed naturally of Easdale slate; competitors get three throws; the stone must bounce at least three times and stay within the designated lane; skims are judged on the distance, not by the number of bounces and the judge's decision is final.

The World Stone Skimming Championships takes place on Easdale Island, Scotland in September each year.

There are competitions for men, women, teams, juniors and in 2009 an 'Old Tossers' category was launched. The World Stone Skimming Cup is presented to the overall winner.

The competition is a fundraiser for the local hall and there is a party there the night before.

The competition was resurrected in 1997 and since then two New Zealanders have claimed the title. In that inaugural event, Ian Sherriff took the title. In 2002 Alastair Judkins became the first person in the history of the event to hit the back wall of the quarry and he claimed a famous victory.

East End Healthy Living Centre

(Formerly Crown Point Sports Complex)
183 Crownpoint Road, Glasgow, G40 2AL
www.eehlc.org.uk

This leisure centre in central Glasgow was host to the World Netball Championships in 1987.

These were to be the last World Championships held outside, so the Silver Ferns had to battle the Scottish elements as well as their opposition.

The 1987 New Zealand Netball team is rated as one of the strongest teams New Zealand has ever put together. Under Coach Lois Muir, and captained by Leigh Gibbs, the Silver Ferns swept all before them.

Right across the team, legends such as Waimarama Taumaunu, Rita Fatialofa, Julie Townsend and Tracey Earl wore the Silver fern with pride.

The team won every match by at least 10 goals. New Zealand beat Trinidad and Tobago in the final and Netball was thrust into a high profile era.

Defender, Tracey Fear remembers: 'I have fantastic memories of 1987. People say it was a team of legends, but you only appreciate the value of the players afterwards.'

In 1999, a New Zealand Dream team was chosen to celebrate 75 years of New Zealand netball. Four of the seven players on the team came from that 1987 World Championship winning side.

Gleneagles

Auchterarder, Perthshire, PH3 1NF
www.gleneagles.com

This luxurious golf and spa resort is set within its own estate in Perthshire, Scotland.

Built in the 1920s, the resort quickly became a stop on the social calendar for high society. It was known as the Highland Riviera.

As well as the three magnificent golf courses, the Gleneagles resort has tennis courts, a day spa, croquet greens and an equestrian school, as well as a shooting and fishing school, falconry, gun dog training and architecture.

Bob Hope said about Scotland: 'The people are so warm and they've got Gleneagles. If only they had the Californian weather I'd move there.'

Today the resort comprises three magnificent golf courses. The King's Course and Queen's Course were both designed by five times British Open champion and renowned golf course architect James Braid. Against a majestic backdrop, the King's Course is seen as the pinnacle of his vast body of work.

Braid has designed some of the UK's best golf courses – such as Carnoustie and Royal Musselburgh. He helped to design over 250 courses across the UK and would have undertaken many more in the USA but he was terrified of flying.

The third course at the resort is the PGA Centenary Course (or Monarch's as it was first known), which was designed by Jack Nicklaus and opened in 1993. Nicklaus is quoted as saying: 'I have always thought Gleneagles is one of the greatest places in the world to play golf.' The course will host the bi-annual Ryder Cup in 2014 between Europe and USA.

It was a team's event on the King's course where New Zealand's Simon Owen celebrated success in 1976. The Double Diamond International was played between countries from 1971 to 1977. The Skol Lager title was given to the leading individual between 1974 and 1977. When Gleneagles hosted the event in 1976, it was Owen who came out on top.

It was in 1976 that Simon Owen won the New Zealand Open at the then newly designed, modern Wellington Golf Course. That 1976 New Zealand Open is also famous because it was when Steve Williams, aged 13 at the time, first caddied in a professional golf tournament. Williams caddied for five-times British Open champion, Peter Thomson, who finished third behind Owen.

It was at Gleneagles where Faldo won his first ever golf tournament – the Skol Lager tournament in 1977.

Gleneagles is a luxurious resort and will linger long in the memory. The golf courses are wonderful, the setting is stunning and the hardest part is saying goodbye.

Inverleith Park

Arboretum Road, Edinburgh, EH3 5NZ
www.inverleithpark.co.uk

The All Blacks played their first ever Test against Scotland at this park in the northern suburbs of Edinburgh.

On 18 November 1905 over 20,000 people watched the All Blacks play Scotland. In a team captained by Dave Gallaher, the All Blacks trailed 7-6 at half-time but on a cold fine day New Zealand came back to win, compliments of a late George Smith try.

The All Blacks celebrated their victory and the Scottish Evening Dispatch described the celebrations as follows:

'... their joy was unrestrained when ultimately they put the issue out of doubt.

The scorer, G.W. Smith, one of the famous men of the side, was embraced, and

literally wept over by his fellows, and if they did not kiss him, well, they came very near to it.'

The Yorkshire Post described the match as: 'A triumph of brains over brawn, of mind over matter'. The latter has been true of many All Blacks v Scotland matches ever since – the men in blue have never beaten the men in black.

It was not just the Scotland team that lost on the day. Scotland's rugby administrators were also big losers. The New Zealanders had wanted a guarantee of £300 for the match but the risk-averse Scottish Rugby Union instead chose to give their guests the net gate receipts instead. This proved to be a poor decision as it became clear in the days before the game how popular the All Blacks were and how the tourists were going to make much more than £300.

Scotland did all they could to ensure the match did not go ahead. They did not put hay on top of the pitch to keep the warmth over night so the ground was hard and slippery because of the ice. The Scottish captain then went to the All Blacks hotel on the morning of the match to say it was off due to a frozen pitch but the All Blacks chose to play on regardless.

This was to be the All Blacks only ever match at Inverleith. Because the All Blacks did not play Scotland on the 1924/25 tour, by the time of New Zealand's next match against Scotland on the 1935-36 tour, Murrayfield had been the home of Scottish rugby for more than 10 years.

Today the park has football and rugby pitches and this green oasis is popular with joggers, sports people and families alike.

Meadowbank Stadium

London Road, Edinburgh, EH7 6AE
www.edinburghleisure.co.uk

This multi-purpose stadium was the host of the Commonwealth Games in 1970 and in 1986. Both the Opening and Closing ceremonies were held here.

In previous Games, the measurements were imperial but in 1970, the Games became metric. The sprint changed from being 100 yards to 100 metres.

In 1970 Les Mills could not defend his 1966 Men's Discus title and finished second. He also finished third in the Shot Put. Dick Quax came in only behind two-time Olympic Gold Medalist Kip Keino in the 1,500 metres. Barbara Poulsen finished second in the Women's Shot Put.

Sixteen years later, again no New Zealander won gold in athletics. Up to and including 2010, this has only happened four times at Commonwealth Games – twice at Meadowbank Stadium and twice in Canada (in Edmonton in 1978 and at Victoria in 1994).

In 1986, Gavin Lovegrove won the first of his three consecutive

Commonwealth bronze medals in the Javelin while Simon Poleman, won a bronze medal in the Decathlon.

That same year, New Zealand's women runners brought further glory. Anne Audain won a silver medal in the 10,000 metres while Lorraine Moller came second in the Marathon.

The athletics events were greatly weakened by the boycott by many of the African and Caribbean countries and came to be known as 'The Boycott Games'.

In 2000 the all glass squash show court was the host for the final stages of the Women's World Open. Australia's Carol Owens beat New Zealand's Lelani Joyce in a five set thriller coming back from two games down. Owens had already moved to live in Auckland and would swap allegiances to play for New Zealand the following year.

Meadowbank Velodrome, Edinburgh

London Road, Edinburgh EH7 6AE
www.edinburghleisure.co.uk

This wooden velodrome in the heart of Edinburgh was home to the track cycling competitions at the British Commonwealth Games in 1970 and the Commonwealth Games in 1986.

It was originally built for the 1970 games and it was on this recently opened track, New Zealand's Harry Kent won a gold medal in the Men's Time Trial. It is true that sport can be about fractions of a second – Kent won by 0.01 seconds. He was given the honour of carrying New Zealand's flag at the closing ceremony.

A month after the games, Kent competed in the World Championships at the Saffron Lane Velodrome in Leicester and finished second in the Kilo Time Trial. For his efforts on the track, Harry Kent was awarded The Halberg New Zealand Sports Person for 1970.

Blair Stockwell also won a medal on the track in 1970 – bronze in the Men's Individual Pursuit.

In 1986 Gary Anderson shone brightly on the track for New Zealand by winning medals in all four track events. Individually he won bronze medals in the Individual Pursuit and the Scratch race and silver in the Time Trial. He then teamed up with Russell Clune, Stephen Swart and Andrew Whitford to claim silver in the 4000 metres team pursuit.

Gary Anderson was only 18 at the time – what a way to introduce yourself to the world. Four years later, when the Games were held in Auckland, Anderson would go on to win three gold medals on the track.

British Olympic hero Sir Chris Hoy trained on the Meadowbank track as a youngster. Today the Velodrome is still used for competitive cycling, but it does not retain its former glory.

Murrayfield

Roseburn Street, Edinburgh, EH12 5PJ
www.scottishrugby.org

The All Blacks have played Scotland 15 times at Edinburgh, and the best the men in blue have ever done is a 0-0 draw in 1964 and a 25 all draw in 1983.

The combined score of All Black matches against Scotland at Murrayfield (up until Rugby World Cup 2011) has been 380-120 or an average of 25-8. Whatever way you look at it, the All Blacks have generally been dominant at the home of Scottish rugby. It's been a black-wash!

Two of those wins were World Cup matches – in 1999 the All Blacks won 30-18 in the quarter-final and in 2007 New Zealand went to Murrayfield and won 40-0 in the group stage.

There is a very special sound at Murrayfield on Test days. Traditional bagpipes, the crowd singing Flower of Scotland, and the roar of the crowd at kick-off.

In 1967 Colin Meads became only the second ever rugby player sent off during a test match (at that time). The All Blacks still won that day 14-3.

The 2005 All Blacks are considered one of the best All Black teams ever. Having swept past the Lions earlier in the year, and won the Tri-Nations, the All Blacks came to the Northern Hemisphere looking to be only the second New Zealand team to do the grand slam. A 29-10 victory over Scotland secured the grand slam and a place in All Black history.

Visitors to Murrayfield always remember the walk to and from the ground. Because the stadium is a mile from the train station and in a residential area, the crowd afterwards tend to walk as a large group and as the All Blacks have won, there is generally a happy mood.

The pubs, bars and restaurants go all out to make the weekend special for visitors to the city. The Royal Mile links Edinburgh Castle to Holyrood Park and the bars and clubs on this stretch are world-renowned.

While traditionally a rugby venue, Murrayfield has hosted some high profile rugby league matches. The rugby league Challenge Cup finals in 2000 and 2002 were played here when the new Wembley Stadium was under construction. In 2000, Bradford beat Leeds 24-18 and Henry Paul was the Man of the Match. Two years later, Wigan beat St Helens 21-12.

The stadium has also hosted pop and rock concerts – everything from David Bowie and the Rolling Stones to Celine Dion and Katherine Jenkins – Highland Games and a visit from His Holiness the Pope.

Raeburn Place, Edinburgh

Portgower Place, Stockbridge, Edinburgh, EH4 1HQ
www.grangecricket.org

On 31 May 1999 New Zealand played Scotland in their final group game of the Cricket World Cup. The home side made a paltry 121 with New Zealand's Chris Harris claiming four wickets from three overs and Geoff Allott took 3/15 from his 10 overs.

New Zealand cruised to their target off 17.5 overs. Roger Twose scored his 50 from 44 balls and New Zealand moved on to the next stage of the tournament.

In the only other World Cup Cricket match played here, Scotland lost to Bangladesh a week earlier.

On the neighbouring field is the Edinburgh Academical Football Club. This club is one of the very oldest rugby clubs in the world and was formed in 1857. Its name excludes the word 'rugby' as the division between the Association and Rugby codes of football happened in the 1860s.

It was on these grounds where the first ever international rugby match took place in March 1871. There were no points at the time, but Scotland scored a goal and a try to beat England's try. The match was 20 players a side and halves were 50 minutes each.

Royal Commonwealth Pool – Edinburgh

Dalkeith Road, Edinburgh, EH16 5BB
www.edinburghleisure.co.uk

The swimming complex was built for the 1970 Commonwealth Games held in Edinburgh and the same venue was used 16 years later when the Games returned to the Scottish capital.

In 1970 Mark Treffers claimed New Zealand's only success in the pool when he won a bronze in the Men's 1,500 metres.

The bounty was much greater the second time around. Anthony Moss was New Zealand's golden boy as he won the 200 metres men Butterfly and a silver medal in the 100 metres Butterfly.

After the games, Moss left New Zealand to study in the USA. He won a bronze medal in the 200 metres Butterfly at the 1988 Seoul Olympics and then two more gold medals in the Commonwealth Games in Auckland in 1990 before retiring from competitive swimming.

Sylvia Hume (now Sinclair) won a gold medal in the Women's 100 metre backstroke. There was yet more success. Paul Kingsman won a pair of silvers in the 100 and 200 metres backstroke. Mike Davidson won bronze in the 400 men's freestyle and Katie Stadlier won New Zealand's first ever medal in Synchronized Swimming; a bronze.

With seven medals, this was New Zealand's most successful games in the pool since the 1974 Games at Christchurch (when the team won eight medals) and only in 1994 and 2006 has it since been matched.

The pool has just undergone a major refurbishment and is now open to the public. The pool will host the diving competition at the 2014 Commonwealth Games.

Royal Highland Centre

Royal Highland Centre, Ingliston, Edinburgh, EH28 8NB
www.royalhighlandcentre.co.uk

This indoor venue was the home to Boxing during the 1986 Commonwealth games in Edinburgh.

New Zealand sent a team of five boxers.

Jimmy 'Thunder' Peau won the heavyweight gold beating local hero Dougie Young in the final with a knockout in the final round. Jimmy Thunder would go on to a professional career winning minor world heavyweight titles.

That same year, in the featherweight division, Johnny Wallace claimed a bronze medal for New Zealand.

In the super heavyweight division, Lennox Lewis won a gold medal for Canada. He went on to win gold at the Seoul Olympics two years later for Canada.

Lewis had been born in London but moved to Canada in his early teens. After the Seoul Olympics in 1988, he switched allegiances to become British again. He became the unanimous heavyweight champion of the world when he beat Evander Holyfield in November 1999 in Las Vegas.

Strathclyde Country Park

366 Hamilton Road, Motherwell , ML1 3ED
www.northlanarkshire.gov.uk

The loch in this country park was the venue for the rowing at the Commonwealth Games in 1986 and for the 1996 World Championships.

It is an artificially created loch, which is one of Scotland's leading tourist attractions for families. On or off the water there is plenty to do such as sailing, playing on the beach, canoe hire, water skiing or relax and have a drink in the café.

It was here on the loch that Stephanie Foster became New Zealand's golden girl of the 1986 games. Along with Robin Clarke she won a gold medal in the Double Sculls and then beat off strong competition to easily win the Single Sculls.

Clarke became only the third New Zealand woman to win two gold medals or more at the Commonwealth Games – after Yvette Williams and Valerie Young. She was nominated for New Zealand Sportsperson of the year but lost out to Sir Richard Hadlee.

New Zealand also won four silvers on the loch in 1986. In both the coxed and coxless fours, New Zealand finished runners-up to England and Canada respectively. Philippa Baker lost by one second in the Lightweight Single Sculls and Barrie Mabbott with Ian Wright finished second in the Coxless Pairs. Eric Verdonk won a bronze medal in the Men's Single Sculls as did the New Zealand Men's Eight.

This was the last Commonwealth Games that included rowing on the programme. Consequently, the Commonwealth Rowing Championships were created and first held in 2002. Strathclyde hosted the event in 2006 and Nathan Cohen won a gold medal for New Zealand in the Men's Single Sculls.

In 2014 the Park will host the Commonwealth Games Triathlon.

The Greenyards – Melrose Rugby Football Club

The Greenyards, Melrose, TD6 9SA
www.melroserugby.bordernet.co.uk

It was here in 1883 that local butcher Ned Haig developed the game of Rugby Sevens. The idea was a fundraiser for the club – as part of a sports day.

Teams were reduced to seven players and matches were only 15 minutes long.

The Greenyards ground nestles beneath the Eildon hills in the Scottish Borders and the small town of Melrose still has a population of fewer than 3,000. On the second Saturday in April it hosts the oldest club sevens tournament in the world with entry today being by invitation.

Both the club and Ned Haig are in the Rugby Hall of Fame and the Rugby World Cup Seven trophy is known today as the Melrose Cup in honour of the club.

Melrose Rugby Club with the Eildon Hills in the background – where Sevens rugby began.

Bay of Plenty returned in 2012 having won the title 20 years previously. Legendary New Zealand Sevens coach, Gordon Teitjens enjoyed his first coaching success at the tournament.

As well as club sevens there is a veterans 10s tournament on the Friday prior and the after party on the Saturday night is renowned in rugby circles.

The Old Course at St Andrews Links

Bruce Embankment, St Andrews, KY16 9XL
www.standrews.org.uk

The Home of Golf – the town is dripping in the history of the game.

The British Open Championship is currently played on the 'Old Course' every five years and in 2010, celebrated the 150th anniversary edition of The Open.

Wherever you look in this famous University town, you are never far from golf-related history, a wide-eyed golfer or golfing merchandise.

Unlike most of the premier courses in the UK, the Old Course at St Andrews Links is officially a public course, but although it is busy there are four main ways to obtain a tee time.

Through the mist is the famous Swilican Bridge on the 17th hole at
St Andrews – British Open 2010.

The famous R & A clubhouse at St Andrews.

Golfers can book in advance with St Andrews Links Trust each September for a tee time in the following year from April to October. Simply download the form from the website and follow the guidelines.

For those who cannot book so far in advance there is a Ballot, or lottery, system in place. Two golfers or more can enter their names before 2pm two days ahead of when they wish to play. The names are drawn and allocated to tee times with the results being posted late afternoon on www.standrews.org.uk. Single golfers can approach the Old Course Starter first thing in the morning to see if he can join them up with two or three-balls.

Finally, tee time packages are available from tour operators including Old Course Experience.

It is possible to play in the winter months, but it can be cold and you will be playing from winter mats. While the 'Old Course' is undoubtedly the most famous course, there are seven different layouts available to play, including The Castle Course on the cliffs overlooking St Andrews, and all of them are great courses.

For golf fans, visiting St Andrews is a pilgrimage. Look back on the Royal and Ancient Clubhouse where the rules of the game are still formed today. Look down the wide first fairway and think of the millions of golf fans who have walked those holes.

Think of the legends of the game – men like Old Tom Morris who used to tend the greens. Or think of his son, Young Tom Morris who won three consecutive Open Championships between 1868 and 1870 and was given the Challenge Belt, which was the prize at the time. There was no Open Championship in 1871 as there was no trophy to give out. When the tournament did return in 1872, Young Tom won again. With the golfing world at his feet, Young Tom Morris, four time Open champion, died only two years later, just 24.

Think about the great triumvirate of J.H. Taylor, Harry Vardon and James Baird who won 16 Opens between them in the 21 Opens from 1894 – 1914. Think about Bobby Jones, the greatest amateur golfer of all who beat the professionals in 1927.

Move forward in time and think about Jack Nicklaus, Arnold Palmer and Gary Player who globalised the game. Nick Faldo won here in 1990. Tip your hat to the late Seve Ballesteros. Tiger Woods set the golfing world alight in 2000, when he was 19 under par and won by eight shots.

Take a walk down to the 17th – the infamous Road Hole where drama has always played out and walk across the Swilcan Bridge. Think about New Zealander Michael Campbell's extraordinary bunker shot in 1995 in the third round when he was the leader going into the final round. Or think about Simon Owen, who when challenging Jack Nicklaus in the final round of The Open in 1978, missed the green, finished on the road and made bogey to hand Nicklaus the title.

It was 18-time Major winner Jack Nicklaus who said: 'Winning at St Andrews was my greatest dream come true.'

But St Andrews is not just famous for the Open Championship. It is also at the heart of the administration of the game. The Royal & Ancient (R & A) still forms the rules today for all golfers. The British Golf Museum across the road from the course is marvellous for history buffs of the game. St Andrew's Links Trust manages the seven courses, including the Old Course, the three clubhouses open to visiting golfers and the state of the art golf academy.

In 1958 the Old Course hosted the first ever Eisenhower Trophy – the premier national team's competition for amateur golfers and the New Zealand team (comprised of Stuart Jones, Bob Charles, John Durry and Ted McDougall) finished fourth. The course also hosted the Commonwealth Tournament, which featured amateur women.

The 2007 Ricoh Women's British Open made history by becoming the first ever professional women's tournament to be played at the 'Home of Golf'. Mexico's Lorena Ochoa was victorious on the Old Course at St Andrews Links.

The Streets of Edinburgh

The Cycling Road race at the 1970 Edinburgh Commonwealth Games took place in heavy rain so the 31 laps around Holyrood Park and the descent down Arthur's seat were treacherous and difficult.

In the tightest of finishes, New Zealand's Bruce Biddle beat Australia's Ray Bilney by a mere inch in a winning time of 4 hours 38 minutes and 6 seconds.

Two years later, Biddle would compete in the 1972 Olympic Road Race in Munich. He finished fourth behind Spain's Jaime Huelamo in another close finish. Subsequently, Huelamo failed a drugs test, but Biddle never received his bronze medal because he had not taken a drugs test.

In 2003 the New Zealand Olympic Committee made a formal request for the medal, but this was turned down.

Huelamo was found to have Coramine (or Nikethamide as it is also known) in his system. The drug was banned by the International Olympic Committee but not by the governing Cycling body.

Turnberry Golf Course

Turnberry Resort, Maidens Road, Turnberry, Ayrshire, KA26 9LT
www.turnberryresort.co.uk

With the famed Turnberry lighthouse in the background, the Ailsa course has hosted Golf's British Open four times.

To golf fans, it is best remembered as the host of the 'Duel in the Sun' in 1977 when Jack Nicklaus and Tom Watson battled in blistering (British) heat over the last two days.

The 9th hole at Turnberry with the Ailsa Lighthouse in the background.

Watson eventually prevailed by a shot and 11 clear of the rest of the field. New Zealander Bob Charles finished down the leader-board in 43rd place that year and Simon Own missed the cut.

In 1986, when Australia's Greg Norman won the first of his two British Opens, Bob Charles turned back the clock finishing 19th. New Zealand's Frank Nobilo finished 59th in the first of his 10 Open appearances.

It was in 1994 that New Zealand golfing spirits were raised as Greg Turner shot a first round 65 to be the first round leader. His sparkling round included an eagle two at the par four 16th hole. He could not keep that pace and eventually finished in 20th. Among those ahead of him was Nobilo who finished 11th. Michael Campbell missed the cut in 1994 and in 2009 when the Open returned to the Ailsa course, withdrew after 12 holes, already 21 over par.

As well as Campbell, in 2009, David Smail and Josh Geary also both missed the cut. It was a bogey on his last hole that cost Geary as he missed playing the weekend by just one shot.

In 2009 it was a bogey on the 18th hole on Sunday, which cost Tom Watson a record equalling sixth Open crown. Instead he lost out to Stewart Cink in the Play-off.

As well as the Open Championship, the course has played host to other major tournaments. Bob Charles won the first of his two Senior British Opens in 1989 with a score of -11.

Seventeen years earlier, Bob Charles also triumphed in the 1972 John Player Classic – at the time the richest golf tournament in Britain.

Westburn Park Bowls Rink

Corn Hill Road, Aberdeen, AB25 3DE
www.aberdeencity.org.uk

In 1984 the Scottish town of Aberdeen hosted the best outdoor bowlers – competing at the World Championships.

New Zealand's Peter Belliss was successful in the men's singles.

Belliss, from Wanganui, beat hometown hero Willie Wood in the final. His victory came on the last bowl – since called 'the perfect bowl' and it came down to an umpire's measure. The comeback was complete as Belliss came back from 18-12 down to win 21-20 and he became the first New Zealand man to ever lift the Singles title.

The Westburn Park rink is still used today, so bowlers can recreate Belliss' famous moment from 1984.

Belliss came from sporting stock. His grandfather Ernest 'Moke' Belliss played 20 games for the All Blacks including three test matches from 1920 to 1923.

The Westburn Park rink was also host to the 2008 World Champion of Champions event won by Kathy Pearce from Wales and Leif Selby from Australia.

ND - #0204 - 270225 - C0 - 234/156/9 - PB - 9781780910581 - Gloss Lamination